FOR EXCELLENT HEALTH DO THIS

A Pharmacist Reveals The 20 Easiest Ways
To Live Longer, Feel Great & Stop Getting Sick

Information For All Readers

This text discusses important concepts related to your health. The work has been checked for accuracy and relevance by licensed health care professionals. However, you should remain aware that this text does not act as a substitute for consultation with a licensed health care expert who can make a proper diagnosis having regard for your unique circumstances.

Copyright © 2023 by LearnWell Books.

All rights reserved. No part of this publication may be reproduced, distributed, or transmitted in any form or by any means, including photocopying, recording, or other electronic or mechanical methods, without the prior written permission of the publisher, except in the case of brief quotations embodied in critical reviews and certain other noncommercial uses permitted by copyright law.

References to historical events, real people, or real places are often fictitious. In such cases, the names, characters, and places are products of the author's imagination. We do this where it's important to protect the privacy of people, places, and things.

689 Burke Rd
Camberwell Victoria 3124
Australia

www.LearnWellBooks.com

We're led by God. Our business is also committed to supporting kids' charities. At the time of printing, we have donated well over $100,000 to enable mentoring services for underprivileged children. By choosing our books, you are helping children who desperately need it. Thank you.

This is really important.
It's a sincere thank you.

My name is Wayne, the founder of LearnWell.

My Dad put a book in my hands when I was 13. It was written by Zig Ziglar and it changed the course of my life. Since then, it's been books that have helped me get over breakups, learn how to be a good friend, study the lives of good people and books have been the source of my persistence through some pretty challenging times.

My purpose is now to return the favor. To create books that might be the turning point in the lives of people around the world, just like they've been for me. It's enough to almost bring me to tears to think of you holding this book, seeking information and wisdom from something that I've helped to create. I'm moved in a way that I can't fully explain.

We're a small and 'beyond-enthusiastic' team here at LearnWell. We're writers, editors, researchers, designers, formatters (oh ... and a bookkeeper!) who take your decision to learn with us incredibly seriously. We consider it a privilege to be part of your learning journey. Thank you for allowing us to join you.

If there's anything we did really well, anything we messed up, or anything AT ALL that we could do better, would you please write to us and tell us (like, right now!) We would love to hear from you!

readers@learnwellbooks.com

We're sending you our thanks, our love and our very best wishes.

Wayne
and the team at LearnWell Books.

WELCOME TO OUR
COMMUNITY

"It's like a private online book club"

 Imagine if you could actually meet and talk with other readers of this book and share your experiences.

 Imagine if you could chat with the author or join them on a live Q&A!

 Imagine getting access to the author's notes and other exclusive, unpublished material.

You can do all of that and a lot more in the LearnWell Online Community!!

→ Download your **Workbook**
→ Chat directly with the author!
→ Meet and feel supported by other readers and their experiences.
→ Access additional, exclusive content about this topic and others.
→ Join our live Author Q&A sessions online.
→ Learn faster, make lasting changes, and have 10 times more fun!

All of this is part of our commitment to creating the best learning resources in the world.

Scan the QR code to get FREE access
www.learnwellbooks.com/healthy

CO-AUTHOR

Our internal team of writers creates our books. We collaborate together, research together, edit each other's manuscripts, and collectively take responsibility for the written work we produce.

Sometimes we will seek input from a subject matter expert who can add meaningful insight on a topic. We interview that expert, often adopt their tone and style and refer to them in the first person. On this occasion, we worked with ...

James Leitman

A pharmacist with the State Primary Healthcare Board. With a Masters in Pharmacology, James has been active in community and hospital practice. As the head of the pharmacy department of the Healthcare Board, James is in charge of counselling patients, ensuring rational drug use, and delivering optimal pharmaceutical services. He has also published several journals, most recently on metformin bioequivalence. When he is not practicing, he enjoys spending time with his wife and playing the guitar.

To Suzie & Will

May you far outlive me and live well

CONTENTS

Recommendations		10
Introduction		12
1	**Your Personal Healthcare Team** How To Put Together The Team That Will Keep You Together	18
2	**Minimizing Downside. Maximizing Results** Be At The Affect Of Your Medications. Not The Mercy.	36
3	**First Aid** Your First Step In Becoming An Everyday Hero	49
4	**Your Kidney and Liver** How You Can Protect These Two Little Heroes	68
5	**Mental and Neurological Disorders** Your Mind Does Matter	78
6	**Your Heart** Tips For A Tip Top Ticker	91
7	**Deadly Diabetes** Three Myths, Two Types Of Diabetes And One Simple Way To Save A Life	105
8	**Managing Your Weight** 4 Reasons To Get In Shape And The Right Way To Do It	121

9	Pain	136
	10 Simple Ways To Manage It	
10	A Happy Pregnancy	145
	... And A Paradox	
11	Caring For Kids	154
	Treating Kids' Health Problems Safely	
12	Coughing & Sneezing	164
	The Causes & Treatments For The Sniffles	
13	Your Largest Organ – Skin	172
	Simple Tips For Healthy Skin	
14	Infections	179
	The 8 Main Types & How To Treat Them	
15	Gut Health	190
	4 Simple Steps To Combat Gut Health Issues	
16	Sexual Health & Healthy Sex	200
	Keeping You In Business	
17	Cancer	214
	Dodge It Or Increase Your Chances Of Beating It	
18	Medical Care Over 65	224
	Managing Pills. Avoiding Spills	
19	Supplements	232
	A Vital Part Of Your Vitality	
20	How To G.R.O.W. Up Healthy	237
	Your Action Plan For Optimal Health	
References		**246**

YOUR
WORKBOOK

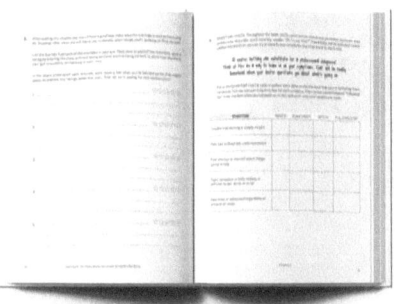

A shocking truth was discovered by a study done in 1987 – **people only remember 10% of what they read!**

That seems so discouraging.

But here's the **GOOD NEWS** – reading is **NEVER** a waste of time. As long as you do **one** important thing ...

The same study (by National Training Laboratories) shows that you will remember 90% of what you read when you **put your new knowledge into action**!

Here at LearnWell, we aim to create **the world's best learning resources**. So, we have included a highly engaging **Workbook** that helps you put your new knowledge into fun, practical action.

So, make sure you download your **FREE Workbook.** You'll find it located inside the **LearnWell Community.** Simply scan the QR code below for access.

Get your Workbook in the LearnWell Community
Scan the QR Code for access or go to:
www.learnwellbooks.com/healthy

RECOMMENDATIONS

I have known James since 2010, and he is an astute and brilliant professional. I was glad to be part of his project on anti-diabetic medications in 2015. I have benefitted from his wealth of experience, especially in the pharmaceutical field, and his large heart. I think books like this, which demystify a lot of medical jargon and help patients understand their health in simple form, are long overdue, and I am proud James has taken the courage to put this body of work together. This is one of the best resources out there for patients and their relatives in improving their health.

Nola Mamora (Pharmacist)

My history with James dates back to 2010. He is well-known for his sound intellectual contributions, questions, and answers. I have had several reasons to seek his opinion on some complex clinical scenarios encountered during my practice. He's one of the few colleagues I have maintained contact with because he's well-read, versatile and always prepared to assist. I have no doubt that this book will be one of your most valued resources for real-life solutions to problems and unanswered questions.

Susan Adani (Pharmacist)

I met James five years ago. Ever since I have known him, he has been very helpful with his professional advice and prescriptions on various health issues. I recommend this book as one of the best resources which any patient and their relatives will find to improve their health.

Owen Simon (Patient)

Recommendations

I have known James for 8 years now and he has been very professional and helpful regarding drug use and practices as well as general health. Safe to say James has become a body of knowledge for me. This resource is a must-read for everyone that puts their health first. The understanding has helped me improve my health and the health of my family.

Eugene Genning (Patient)

INTRODUCTION

"What do you think, James? Does his eye look like it's getting better to you?"

The woman gave her child a gentle shove in the back. He reluctantly stepped forward and lifted his face towards me. His eye looked reddish and swollen. If anything, it was worse than the last time she'd brought him in to get his prescription filled.

"I've been applying his eye drops every day for the past couple of weeks, just as the doctor said, but it doesn't seem to be helping."

"And you told the doctor this?"

"Yes." The woman sighed. "He said to keep going, and eventually it would clear up. I suppose you'd better give us more drops. The doctor wouldn't have prescribed them if they weren't going to work, would he?" She handed me the prescription.

"Hmmm." I read the doctor's notes. The child had been prescribed corticosteroid eye drops. While they can work wonders when used correctly, continued use beyond a week can do more harm than good.

I gave her back the prescription. "I'm not a doctor," I told her, "but if I were you, I'd get a second opinion. I'll give you the drops if you want, but you might be better off waiting to see what someone else says."

Introduction

A couple of days later, the woman was back. "Thank you so much for telling me to get a second opinion," she said. "The other doctor told me that the eye drops were the wrong treatment. He says this should do the trick."

She gave me a new prescription and I filled it for her. The next time she came into my pharmacy, her little boy was with her.

"And how are you doing, young man?" I asked, giving him a lollipop from the stash on the counter.

"Absolutely fine now," she beamed, as her son busied himself unwrapping the candy. "He just needed different eye drops. His eye cleared up within a couple of days after that."

I see it time and again. So many people suffering from debilitating conditions or side effects from medication, and all because they take one doctor's opinion as the ultimate truth and don't know which questions to ask.

It might shock you to know that out of every 100 deaths, 74 are due to non-communicable diseases, i.e. diseases which cannot be transmitted from one person to another, such as cancer or heart disease. Seven out of the 10 global leading causes of death are noninfectious diseases[1]. Most of these are chronic diseases. That's according to the World Health Organization (WHO).

These diseases are killing more and more people each year. The chances are high you know someone who has died from one of the biggest killers: heart disease, stroke, respiratory disease, cancer, dementia, diabetes, and kidney disease.

It's a sobering thought, especially since we know that many of these conditions can be managed with lifestyle changes and medication. Sadly, while modern medicine can prolong our lives, many people with these conditions don't enjoy a good quality of life. They live with pain and disability every single day.

For some of these people, their disease progressed too far before they realized there was a problem. But for others, the problem lay with suboptimal treatment and a failure of that treatment. Why does this happen?

It might be because the patient isn't taking their medications as prescribed. Or, they may be taking the wrong medication or a placebo. Another possibility is that they may suffer from adverse reactions to a drug, which makes them understandably reluctant to take it.

While these are all avoidable, when a problem occurs, it isn't always the doctor or patient's fault. There may have been a miscommunication or misunderstanding. A doctor can only act with the information they are given. Conversely, a patient won't always know which details are essential. Or, they might not know the right questions to ask to get the information *they* need. The relationship between healthcare professional and patient requires a delicate balance - and it's the patient who will have to live with the consequences of any decision.

It's a sobering thought.

If ill-health should strike, you'll want to be certain your medications won't fail you. Sure that you don't have to visit the doctor too

Introduction

often. Confident that you're getting the greatest benefit out of the medicine your doctor gives you.

What can you do to get the very best medical care at all times?

So many questions and things to consider at a time when all you want to do is focus on the most important thing: your health.

This book will tackle all these questions and more. You'll be reassured to know that by the time you've finished reading, you'll be equipped with everything you need to get the best out of your healthcare professionals. You'll learn:

- How to minimize adverse effects from your medications
- How to cooperate with your healthcare provider when taking your meds
- How to keep an accurate, helpful record of your health to support your doctor or pharmacist to give you the right drugs
- How to use this record to lower the chances of being given inappropriate drugs
- The danger signs to watch out for with some of the more serious conditions
- Basic first aid techniques which could save your life.

You hold in your hands a guide you can come back to time and again whenever you're faced with a health problem. The best thing to do is read through the whole book first to get an overview of how to take responsibility for your health. You can then come back to read the most pertinent chapters when you need. Alternatively, if you're in urgent need of support, you may want to to turn to the chapter that is most relevant to your current situation and come back to the rest later. However you use this book, consider it an important step on your journey towards your best health!

I want to stress that this book is not intended to replace professional advice. Everyone's situation is unique, and you should always consult a qualified physician if you have any doubts or concerns. What this book will do is arm you with the information you need to make the job of your healthcare providers easier. I'll take you through the right questions to ask to ensure your doctor fully understands your particular problem. I'll also teach you how to use your medication effectively.

Sounds good?

"Yes, but where's the catch?" you might be thinking. *"Why should I trust you?"*

As a fully qualified, practicing pharmacist, I've dealt with countless people suffering from serious health issues which were otherwise preventable. There's nothing more heartbreaking than trying to help someone who has a threatening condition as a result of the mismanagement of their health. Prevention is always better than the cure. While we might not be able to avoid every negative in life, we can most certainly put the odds in our favor.

It is my hope that this book will empower you to take charge of your health. My aim is to guide you into having more productive discussions with healthcare professionals, so they can help you make better decisions about your health. They have a lot to teach you. This book will help you make the most of their extensive knowledge. You will be able to tell your doctor about your condition in a way that makes it easier for them to treat you effectively.

As a pharmacist, I've supported people to make small changes when dealing with their doctor to get big results. These little tweaks have helped many people to drastically improve their health and quality of life, even with chronic ailments. Now I'm sharing them with you.

By taking the small steps outlined in this book, you'll have the confidence to take full responsibility for your health. You'll be able to start having productive discussions with your healthcare providers to fully understand the implications of every decision you make, so you can make the best choices for your personal circumstances. This will minimize the risk of your requiring unnecessary treatment or suffering side effects from the wrong medication.

It's time to take charge of your health. Read this book, follow its advice, and start having productive discussions with your healthcare providers.

I wish you a happy, wealthy, and most importantly, healthy life.

James Leitman

Pharmacist, LearnWell Subject Expert

YOUR PERSONAL HEALTHCARE TEAM

How To Put Together The Team That Will Keep You Together

*A truly great doctor is hard to find,
difficult to part with, and impossible to forget.*

– unknown

Here's a great starting question "How do I find my medical team?"

The good news is I'm here to help! In this chapter, you'll find all the knowledge you need. You'll learn how to find a thoughtful, capable medical team that accommodates your needs. I'll guide you to think about your personal criteria and priorities. You can then use this to identify which professionals are the right fit for you. By following the information in this chapter, you can be confident that your needs will always be met.

I'll never forget the time I made a woman cry in the middle of my pharmacy.

She'd come in to refill her heart medication, but when she started to count out her change, she discovered she was a dollar short.

"It's okay," she sighed as she pushed the pill bottle back across the counter to me. Her hand shook a little, and she struggled to look me in the eye. "I still have a few pills left at home. I'll make them last until my son comes over with some money."

I frowned. "How are you going to do that?"

"Oh, you know. They say doctors prescribe more pills than you need because they're just trying to make more money. I often cut back on how many pills I take if I don't have the money for more. It doesn't do me any harm."

I looked at the bottle. How could I gently tell her the truth? "These are beta blockers. If you don't take them properly, you could cause yourself a heart attack."

The woman went pale. For a moment, I worried she was going to have a heart attack right there and then. "But..." Her bottom lip quivered. "This is all the money I have. I'm going to have to get my son to pay for my medication, and I don't know when that will be."

"A dollar short, you said?"

The woman nodded.

"Well, it just so happens that today I'm offering a dollar discount on beta blockers. Looks like you've got just the right amount."

The woman burst into tears, barely able to get her purse out because she was sobbing so hard.

"It's okay," I told her. "You're doing me a favor. I wouldn't be able to sleep tonight if you didn't have your pills. I'd be too worried about what might happen to you."

"You don't understand," she sobbed. "Nobody's ever done this for me before. When I've been in the same position before, I've had pharmacists tell me I was lying. I've worked hard all my life. I'd never try to steal a dollar from anyone!"

"Well, whoever those pharmacists are, they've just lost a great customer, haven't they?" I rang up her prescription, and the smile through her tears was beautiful.

Too often, medical professionals assume their patients are medically literate. Unfortunately, most people aren't! No one should have to risk their health because they haven't been told the risks associated with not taking their medication. I'll never forget that woman. She was clearly struggling financially and was risking her life in the process. Sadly, the medical system isn't designed for people who don't have extra dollars to spare.

That's why it's important to identify your priorities when searching for the right medical team. You need to be surrounded by people you can trust. People with whom you can share your struggles and who will make sensible and safe changes to overcome them.

Taking charge of your health starts right here.

Begin to see your healthcare professionals as part of your own team. A team working together for your benefit, with you as the captain. You are in charge of this human vessel, so it's up to you to staff it with the right people.

Keep in mind that the team you develop depends on your personal needs, and that these needs will change over time. . For example, when you have children, you'll need to find a pediatrician. If you develop a health problem later in life, such as diabetes or heart disease, you'll want to work with a specialist in your condition.

Your team might include some of these professionals:

- General Practitioners
- Pharmacists
- Nurses
- Physiotherapists
- Osteopaths

FOR EXCELLENT HEALTH DO THIS

- Exercise Physiologists
- Massage Therapists
- Dentists
- Cardiologists
- Podiatrists
- Dietitians
- Psychologists
- Chiropractors
- Optometrists
- Speech Pathologists
- Pediatric Specialists
- Spiritual and Social Support Providers
- Rehabilitation Specialists
- Administrative and Support Staff

At first, the team building process might seem a little daunting. After all, you'll need to do this with each medical professional. However, as you venture into the process and begin to take ownership of your health, I'm confident you'll find it rewarding.

As I say to my customers, a couple of hours spent at the start of your professional relationship can save a broken heart (or bones!) further down the line. Taking the time to do this now will reassure you that your team have your back. You'll have the confidence to discuss any problems, no matter how trivial. You'll know you can ask the questions you want to get the information you need.

Sound good? Then let's start the process of assembling your team …

 In your Workbook, you'll find a directory that will provide you with a single place to keep information about your medical team. You'll find a copy at learnwellbooks.com/healthy

Although this is information related to your medical team, let the LearnWell Community be a part of your social support as we continue.

YOUR RIGHTS AS A PATIENT

Before choosing anyone to work on something as important as your health, you need to know that they respect your rights. They are typically bound to do so by law, but how individual healthcare professionals interpret that law may vary.

Whilst your legal rights will depend on your location, the following rights are generally considered universal:

> **The right to know what drug you are being prescribed.**
> There's a big difference between Clobazam, which is used to treat epilepsy, and Clonazepam, which is an antianxiety medication. Understanding exactly what you're taking and having the confidence to question whether it's the right drug for you can avoid nasty side effects. 251,000 American deaths annually can be accounted for through medical

errors[2]. These would otherwise be preventable deaths if patients knew to question their prescription.

The right to know which adverse reactions or damage you may experience following the use of a drug. Up to the frightening number of 40,000 Americans die every year due to side effects of their medication.[3] When you're aware of the risks of a particular drug, you can make an informed choice as to whether you want to take it or deal with your problem differently. Sometimes, the cure really is deadlier than the disease.

The right to decide against taking a particular drug and request an alternative. Given the above statistics, are you so sure you just want to do what your doctor advises? Many doctors, whether they're aware of it or not, are being incentivized to prescribe certain drugs over others. A study by the *New England Journal of Medicine* investigated the issue of doctors receiving money from big pharma.[4] An incredible 94% reported some form of relationship with the pharmaceutical industry. These may seem innocuous - pharmaceutical companies might supply drug samples, pay for trials, pay a physician to give a lecture, or reimburse the cost of continuing medical education (CME). These are all wonderfully magnanimous and seem to have nothing to do with encouraging a doctor to favor their medications. But these interactions help doctors save money and further their career, which fosters a feeling of gratitude and may cause doctors to want to return the favor. Furthermore, by covering the cost of CME, pharmaceutical companies may even control the information a doctor receives about certain treatments. This is why it's so important to review what you're being prescribed and ask about alternatives.

The right to be treated with respect and dignity at all times, including protection from rudeness or inappropriate behavior. According to a report carried out by the Federation of State Medical Boards, almost 1 in 5 Americans have suffered misconduct by their physician, yet few report the behavior or file a complaint.[5] I know that when you've been mistreated by a physician, it can be difficult to find the strength to report them. Even if you don't feel like you can speak up, you need to know that it's not okay. It's always okay to change the members in your medical team for any reason.

The right to confidentiality. There are some exceptions to this. For example, your confidentiality can be broken if a medical professional deems you to be a danger to yourself or others. This can be confusing. You may be asking yourself, "What constitutes being a 'danger to others?'". You're not the only one who's asked this question, so here's some clarity! If you have a condition that is hazardous to public health, your medical team may need to make a statement to public health officials. If your injuries are suggestive of criminal activity, the medical team may be required to report them to legal authorities. If your injuries are suggestive of self-harm or of immediate danger to your person, they may be required to break confidentiality and report it. When you're the patient of an interdisciplinary team, you can often expect the members of the team to share the information you provide with each other, unless you've been told otherwise. If you find yourself in one of these situations, you should always be made aware that your details are being shared.

The right to legal action following negligence. A 2011 study published in the *New England Journal of Medicine* found that 75% of physicians in 'low-risk' specialities and virtually all physicians in 'high-risk' specialities would face at least one malpractice claim during their career.[6] 73% of settled malpractice claims surrounded medical error. While you should always consult a lawyer before making the decision to launch an expensive, time-consuming and often traumatic claim, you should also be aware that you are entitled to compensation if your doctor has been negligent.

It is always worth taking the time to find out the complaints' procedure so that you're aware of what to do if your rights are infringed. To do this, contact your healthcare provider to ask about their process and determine who you can complain to. In other circumstances, you may need to take your issue to the hospital administrator or regional licensing board.

You should always feel supported in bringing a complaint to the appropriate authorities if necessary. If you feel that your healthcare professionals are not respecting your rights, do not be afraid to find someone who will. (More on that in a moment.)

Any healthy relationship should be reciprocal. Just as you have rights and expectations, so does your medical team. As discussed before, the details regarding your rights will vary depending on your location. Take the time to find out what you're entitled to in your locale. (Ask your team to signpost you to information if you need.) Knowing your rights may also impact on the quality of your treatment. Knowledge is power. Knowing what you can and can't expect will support you to stand up for what you need.

For example, in some locations, healthcare professionals may choose not to treat you based on their personal religious opinions or beliefs. A pro-life doctor may be protected from offering abortion services in your area. At the time of writing, 46 states in the United States have passed legislation protecting medical professionals from performing abortions if it goes against their religious beliefs[7]. Now that Roe vs. Wade has been overturned, it is possible that more changes have been made to local legislation. Do your research to find out what this means for you.

This also means that you may not be able to sue for medical negligence if a doctor refuses to provide medical care that contradicts their religious opinions. It's important to find out whether this applies to your choice of medical professional so that you understand the possible implications.

While it can be frustrating not to have your first choice of doctor, if you find yourself in this situation, ask yourself whether you really want to work with a medical professional who doesn't share your attitudes.

When a healthcare professional gives you their advice, you are more than entitled to ask for further information about their recommendation. You can also decide you don't want to follow their advice. It's your health and your decision. If you do decide not to follow medical advice, make sure you have all the information required before doing so. You can always seek out a second or third professional opinion if you want more information that isn't provided by your current medical professional. By knowing as much as possible about your situation, you can be an active participant in your health and can make decisions in consideration of all risks and benefits.

FINDING YOUR HEALTHCARE DREAM TEAM

"Can I ask you a question?"

I looked up to see who was talking to me. The man looked to be in his early sixties. His clothes were neat but worn, and he had an air about him which suggested he wasn't used to speaking out. He meandered through the aisles, seeming unsure of what he might be looking for, until he hesitantly approached me.

"Of course you can. I'm here to help!" I smiled reassuringly.

"I'm new to the area and I need to find a doctor," he said. "I've got this problem with my back and..." He shrugged. "Well, I don't need to trouble you about it, but I could use a doctor to check it out."

It's a common scenario. People find themselves needing to build their healthcare team from scratch, but aren't sure how to go about it. Maybe they're new to an area and don't have any contacts, or maybe their partner used to deal with details like that, but they're no longer around.

Fortunately, there's a simple process you can use. I talked the man through it and when I was done, he had a smile from ear to ear.

"Thank you so much!" he said. "I tell you something - I might not have found a new doctor yet, but I know who my pharmacist is!"

What did I say that made him so happy? I gave him these straightforward steps:

Personal referrals are always the best way to find someone. Start by asking neighbors, family and friends for their recommendations.

If you don't have any personal recommendations, the internet is your friend! Search for doctors in your area (or whatever medical personnel you need) and then search for reviews on the practitioner you're interested in. Also, check whether your insurance covers them.

Contact the medical professional you're thinking of working with. It's worth interviewing a potential provider either in person or over the phone. Some practitioners will offer this for free, while others may require you to schedule a visit. Ask about their approach and services. If you've had problems with doctors not listening to you in the past, the best thing to do is sound them out over the phone and see if they appear genuinely interested in treating your problem. You could also ask how many years they've been specializing in a particular field. And a little word of advice - if they say you need a procedure, ask how many they've completed and what their success rate is.

Other useful questions include: Does the clinic staff specialize in any other health area you're concerned about? Their website might mention they do, but it would still be useful to hear about this from them first hand. Also, ask questions which seem obvious but are really valuable when it comes to determining their attitude towards patients, like: Who answers the phone when I call the clinic with questions? How long would I have to wait for an appointment for urgent care? How long for a physical? What are your opening hours? What do I do if I have a problem out of hours? Who do I see if my primary provider isn't available?

Don't rush into making a decision. After your initial consultation, think about whether the provider really listened to you and whether you'd feel comfortable discussing your health problems with them. Do you think they'd respect your decisions? Did they welcome questions and answer them in a way that made sense to you? And, most importantly, do you feel like you could trust them?"

These and other helpful questions are included in your Workbook with a table for you to keep a record of the answers from each professional. Access your Workbook at learnwellbooks.com/healthy

Remember, if you've got any doubts or concerns about a healthcare professional, don't be afraid to keep looking until you find one which is a better fit. This is your health at stake. You deserve someone who will look after you.

ESTABLISHING AND MAINTAINING RELATIONSHIPS WITH HEALTHCARE PROFESSIONALS

Here's a very simple principle that will keep your team on side: Treat your healthcare professionals the way you'd like to be treated.

Remember, there will always be a professional boundary in your relationship. They're a medical professional, not your friend. Maintaining that distance is what helps them to remain objective and give you the best possible advice. As much as you might want to show them photos of your adorable new puppy, they're there to discuss your health, not your furry family.

Be friendly, but respect their boundaries.,

> **Don't contact them after hours** - they need their beauty sleep too!
>
> **Don't make small talk** - keep discussions on topic.
>
> **Prepare questions in advance** - don't be afraid to make a list of the things you need to discuss and refer to it during your meeting. Your medical professional will appreciate your preparedness and you'll have the reassurance of knowing you won't forget anything.
>
> **Don't take up more of their time than you need** - think about how you feel when you're kept waiting for an appointment because they're running late. If you want to be respected, show respect for their time.

As I tell my customers, working in healthcare is a vocation. We don't do this job for the money. We don't do it for any glory. Still, it's always an added bonus when someone shows they value your help. Showing your healthcare professional respect is the ultimate in appreciation!

If you've got a suggestion about your health, whether that's because of something you've read in this book or information you've found elsewhere, pose it as a question:

- "I read an article about treatment vaccines for cancer. Can you tell me about the relevance of those for me?"
- "I heard that inclisiran is a good way to bring down blood cholesterol. Can you share your experience with it and how appropriate it would be for my condition?"
- "I'm worried I'm suffering from postpartum depression. My friend had an intravenous treatment, which she said really helped. Could I have that, and, if not, what are my alternatives?"

Whatever you've read or researched, be open-minded about your doctor's response. No amount of research is a true substitute for professional advice. Be aware that opinions can vary. Even when you've looked into official guidelines from organizations such as the CDC or WHO, these guidelines are open to individual, professional interpretation.

AFTER YOUR APPOINTMENT

As soon as you leave your appointment, try to book the next one. Ask: *"Can I see the same doctor or pharmacist?"* Every healthcare provider is obliged to keep accurate records about your condition. However, if you can, see the same person at every appointment. This is the best way to ensure consistency of approach to your healthcare.

MAKING CHANGES TO YOUR TEAM

Now you know how to build your dream team of healthcare professionals. However, there will be times when you will need to switch up your team. For example you might need to replace a particular person (e.g. they're relocating, or you don't want to work with them) or you need to put together a new team (e.g. you're relocating).

Unless your relationship is beyond repair, it's always a good idea to ask your existing team for a referral. If you work well with your current team, the chances are high you would work well with someone they recommend. Otherwise, go through the previous steps outlined in this chapter to find a replacement.

If it is not your choice to find a new team member, finding a replacement can be disheartening. Be open to new possibilities. You may find you end up loving your new healthcare provider.

Even if you've had some negative experiences, it's important to remember that the vast majority of healthcare providers want the best for their patients. You will find a good alternative.

It's time to shift your mindset from one of seeing medical professionals as an integral part of your healthcare regime. *They* work for *you!*

Think of your health as being like a beautiful garden and you its caretaker. It is up to you to weed it, water it, and nourish the soil, so the flowers can bloom.

FOR EXCELLENT HEALTH DO THIS

Your healthcare team is there to give you the support you need to help with tasks you can't handle for yourself. If a tall tree needed pruning, you'd bring someone in with the specialist tools and skills to cut it back safely to enable the rest of the garden to thrive, but most of the time, you know what it takes to maintain your garden.

Your health is the same. You're the one who is ultimately responsible for staying fit and well. Your healthcare professionals should respect that and support you to find the best solution to your problems when they occur. They should deal with you as an individual and not just another case study.

Remember that this garden, your health, needs a team to ensure it truly flourishes. Each part of the team has an important role to play, and you all have rights which need to be respected. When everyone's happy with their working relationship, you'll be able to have confidence in your team.

Make it your practice to interview any potential provider before you decide to work with them. Use the suggested questions I talked about when interviewing new members of your team to see whether they share your outlook on healthcare. If you don't feel that you can have a positive relationship with them, keep looking. This is potentially one of the most important decisions you can make. It could quite literally mean the difference between life and death.

Once you've built your team, it's time to make sure your medications are working as hard for you as your doctor and pharmacist do. In the next chapter, we'll be examining how to minimize adverse reactions from your drugs. After all, your garden won't grow if you're using the wrong kind of plant food for your flowers! You'll learn about the common mistakes people make with their medications, sometimes with devastating effect. I'll give you everything you need to know to avoid making them so you don't become another health statistic.

 If you haven't done so yet, take a moment to become familiar with your new Workbook. It's full of helpful resources that relate to this chapter. Get your copy at learnwellbooks.com/healthy

MINIMIZING DOWNSIDE. MAXIMIZING RESULTS

Be At The Affect Of Your Medications. Not The Mercy.

It is very expensive to give bad medical care to poor people in a rich country.

– Paul Farmer

If I could only give my customers one piece of advice, it would be to make sure they understand the possible side effects of any medication, whether it's bought over the counter or prescription only.

There is no such thing as a drug that doesn't have a potential adverse effect. And if you aren't aware of them, you may find that the cure can be worse than the disease.

I'm always filled with respect for people who join studies - it's how we learn more about whether a drug will do what we want it to do, after all.

But, in some instances, that study might not have been such a good thing. Fun fact - this actually happens with a lot of my customers! People don't always react well to their medications, with sometimes surprising effects.

Take the man with diabetes who signed up to a study to see whether taking statins (a cholesterol-lowering drug) might help his condition. His wife came into my pharmacy to fill his most recent script. While I was serving her, she confided in me that she was increasingly concerned about her husband.

"He used to be such a sweet person," she told me. "But ever since he started on these drugs, he's become so *angry*. It's gotten so bad that he's given up driving, which is why I'm getting his medication for him. He got involved in a terrible argument with someone the other day because they didn't pull away the second the lights turned red. If I'm honest, I'm a little afraid of him."

"That's awful." I shook my head. "Have you spoken to the people running the study about it?"

"We tried." She sighed. "They weren't interested. They told us there was no way the drugs were causing his anger and the best thing to do was keep taking the pills and stay in the study."

"Hmmm." I frowned. "Well, I'm not a doctor and I can't tell you what to do, but if I were you, I'd speak with another practitioner about it."

A few weeks later, I saw the woman again.

"How's your husband?" I asked.

She laughed. "We took your advice and tried talking to the organizers of the study again. When they repeated that he should keep taking the pills, he got really annoyed. He yelled at them before storming out, saying he'd never take another pill again. He was so mad, he kept his word. Ironically, being angry made all the difference. A couple of weeks later, I had my lovely husband back. The temper was all gone. Who'd have thought pills to treat diabetes could have such an effect?"

Who, indeed.

In fact, there is plenty of documented evidence to support the fact that statins can cause behavioral changes in some people - and it's not the only drug to have this effect. For example, acetaminophen (or paracetamol) may lower your ability to feel compassion[8].

Now, this doesn't mean you should immediately stop taking your pills. Always check with a medical professional before making that kind of decision. But when you are aware of the potential side effects of a medication, you can make an informed choice about whether it's the right choice for you - and you can stop taking it if you become aware that it's causing you problems.

ADVERSE REACTIONS VS SIDE EFFECTS

You may hear your doctor talking about adverse reactions or side effects. You may even think these are the same things. However, there's an important difference between the two, and understanding this could save your life.

An **adverse reaction** is a negative, undesirable occurrence resulting from correctly taking your medications. There are two types: Type A reactions are predictable, usually dose dependent, and can be mild, moderate, or severe; Type B are unpredictable and have nothing to do with dose. These are rarer and are generally influenced by the patient's circumstances, such as drug allergies.

A **side effect** is a negative occurrence that has no connection to dosage and is usually predictable. In fact, sometimes, a drug's side effects may be the reason why it's prescribed. For example, patients suffering from anorexia may be prescribed medications causing weight gain. You should be warned about the possibility of a side effect, which will generally resolve given time.

It's important you report any potential issue with a drug to your pharmacist or doctor to determine whether your medication really is the problem. If, like my customer's husband, you're initially told there's no connection, but you feel there is, don't be afraid to seek a second opinion for reassurance.

THE IMPORTANCE OF YOUR WORKBOOK

One way you can identify side effects is by keeping your Workbook up to date. This Journal will make the work of your healthcare professionals easier because they'll have a full picture of your health history.

Open your Workbook now so that you're familiar with it. It should contain:

- Your personal details, such as name, age, sex, etc.

- Any pertinent family medical history of chronic diseases such as hypertension, diabetes, asthma, cancer, etc. Also, note whether any family member died as a result of their condition.

- Your personal medical history, such as chronic conditions like asthma, diabetes, kidney disease, liver, disease, etc. Note when you were diagnosed with that condition. Additionally, record any acute conditions like colds, flu, infections, etc.

- Write down any medications you take, including over the counter, prescription only and complementary remedies. Document when you started taking these and when you stopped (if you've stopped at all).

- Document when you travel, especially if you go to areas prone to diseases like malaria or dengue fever.

- Include any known allergies or genetic conditions that can affect your reaction to medications. Detail previous reactions.

- Note if you're pregnant or breastfeeding.

Keeping your Workbook makes it very easy for a medical professional to figure out the most appropriate medication. An added bonus is that you'll be able to identify side effects early - if my customer's husband had been recording his medications and moods, he might have noticed the correlation sooner. Likewise, it'll help you see whether something is an actual reaction or mere coincidence. It might be that your drugs are giving you a stomach ache, or maybe it was that very large Thanksgiving dinner you had!

THE TYPES OF ADVERSE REACTIONS

Be aware of potential adverse reactions, so you know what to look out for. If you have any concerns at all, speak to your doctor (or friendly neighborhood pharmacist!) to determine whether your issue is related to your medication or there's another cause.

Check the drug insert for the likelihood of adverse reactions. There are six different types of adverse reactions:

> **Augmented** reactions are the result of an exaggeration of a drug's normal effect when administered at the usual dose. So, if you were prescribed warfarin, you might experience bleeding. These reactions may also include known side effects that aren't directly related to the aim of the drug, such as someone experiencing a dry mouth when taking tricyclic antidepressants.

Bizarre reactions are unexpected reactions to a drug and are less common, so they may only become apparent after a drug has been approved for general use. One example is an individual suffering anaphylaxis after taking penicillin, or getting a skin rash while taking antibiotics.

Continuous or chronic reactions continue for a relatively long time, such as when someone develops osteonecrosis of the jaw following a course of bisphosphonates.

Delayed reactions can be difficult to detect because they occur a while after someone has started taking their medication. For example, lomustine, a chemotherapy drug, can result in leukopenia (low white blood cell count) up to six weeks after receiving a dose.

End-of-use reactions occur when someone stops taking medication, like when someone experiences insomnia, anxiety, and hallucinations when ceasing to take benzodiazepines.

Failure of treatment reactions are when a drug doesn't have the expected effect. This might be caused by too low a dose being prescribed or a patient not taking the medication as prescribed.

AVOIDING AN ADVERSE REACTION

It can be a pretty scary place when you start going down the rabbit hole of adverse reactions. You'll wonder why anyone ever takes any medications at all! But there's a lot you can do to minimize the chances of your experiencing a negative side effect. Here's a few ways:

Always ask your doctor or pharmacist about the side effects of any drug. At the very least, they should be able to tell you about the most common problems, so you know what to watch out for.

Read the leaflet accompanying your medication. This details everything you need to know. It will list all known adverse reactions, including rare ones your doctor may not have had time to warn you about.

Ask your doctor or pharmacist if you should avoid any specific food or drink. Milk, coffee, tea, and alcohol are commonly associated with reactions. For example, if you're prescribed ciprofloxacin, you may experience treatment failure if you take it with milk or antacids. Likewise, alcohol is a known problem with many drugs, such as metronidazole and omeprazole.

Tell your doctor or pharmacist if you're taking any other drugs or supplements. Ask whether additional medications may interfere with them. Just because something's natural doesn't mean it's safe, and some supplements can interfere with your medications. St. John's Wort, for example, is known to negatively impact a number of different drugs, such as warfarin, some HIV protease inhibitors, or anticonvulsants. Likewise, some medications cannot be taken together, such as some birth control pills and antibiotics. Antibiotics may render your birth control ineffective.

Never self-medicate. As a little addendum to the previous point, don't be tempted to self-medicate if your drugs aren't working the way you would like them to. Take any concerns back to the appropriate medical professional. Otherwise, you risk causing yourself more harm.

Tell your doctor or pharmacist if there's any family history of issues with certain drugs. Even if you haven't personally experienced a problem, genetics are known to be an issue when it comes to how your body processes medications, and it may be that an alternative is more suitable for you.

Check the dosage of your medication. Many reactions are associated with incorrect dosage, so make sure you've been given the right amount.

Make sure you know how to take your medication. The best way to avoid an adverse reaction due to patient error is to not make a mistake in the first place! Check how often you should be taking your medication and in what amount - set an alert on your phone to remind yourself if you need. Your Workbook will be helpful for this.

Report any unintended effect of your medications to your doctor. It may be coincidental, but your doctor will be in a good position to know whether you should have concerns or not. If you do not feel your doctor is taking you seriously, you may be able to self-report side effects to the appropriate organization, such as FAERS (FDA Adverse Event Reporting System) in the US or the Yellow Card Scheme in the UK.

Get yourself to rehab if you have an addiction. Not only is it a good idea to get professional help for your condition regardless, illegal drugs can interfere with some medications.

WHAT TO DO WHEN YOU SUFFER AN ADVERSE REACTION

If you've taken the time to educate yourself about potential side effects of your medications, you'll be in a better position to identify them if you're unlucky enough to experience one. It may be that the benefits of the drug outweighs the risks, so you can't know whether something will be a problem until you try.

In the first instance, speak to your doctor. Don't just stop taking your medications without discussion. It may be that the reaction is temporary and will pass as your body adjusts. Some drugs, such as antibiotics, need you to take the full course for them to be effective. Others won't work as well if you miss a dose or deliberately take less than prescribed.

It may also be that you can make simple changes to deal with the side effects. For example, birth control pills may make you dizzy, so try taking them before bed, so you don't notice the impact of them.

Some more serious side effects may require immediate medical attention. Often, these occur soon after taking the drug, such as an allergic reaction. Anaphylaxis can be serious, even fatal. The symptoms include, feeling faint, struggling to breathe, increased heart rate and anxiety. If you suspect anaphylaxis, the individual needs hospital treatment as quickly as possible, Use an adrenaline injector if you have one and call emergency help immediately.

Check the drug leaflet for any serious adverse reactions and familiarize yourself with the signs and symptoms so you can get early intervention if you are unfortunate enough to suffer a severe reaction.

YOU ARE YOUR BEST EARLY WARNING SYSTEM

You picked up this book because you wanted to know how best to care for your health. It is ultimately your responsibility to ensure you're taking your drugs correctly. Accidental acetaminophen (paracetamol) overdose is the leading cause for calls to Poison Control Centers, accounting for over 100,000 calls a year. It necessitates over 56,000 emergency room visits, 2,600 hospitalizations and a tragic 458 deaths every year[9]. These deaths could have been avoided had the individuals concerned been more aware of how to take this common, over the counter drug.

When your doctor or pharmacist instructs you on how to take your medications, get into the habit of repeating what they've said in your own words to confirm that you've understood what they're telling you. Not only does this help you to remember what you're supposed to do, it gives them the opportunity to correct you if you've misunderstood anything.

Many branded drugs are available in a generic form, which is just as effective but at a fraction of the cost. Don't be afraid to ask if there's an alternative version of the medication you're being prescribed, and remember to show your healthcare professional all the meds you're currently taking, so they don't prescribe anything which might be contraindicated.

ASK FOR HELP

Following this simple acronym can support you to take more responsibility for your medication.

- H - **How** many pills have you been given? Do you have enough for your course of treatment? For example, if you've been told to take two pills twice a day for ten days, you'll need forty pills.

- E - When are your pills **expiring**? Medications don't last forever, and taking pills which are past their shelf life can be dangerous. Take any out of date drugs back to your pharmacist for appropriate disposal.

- L - What is the **label** of your meds? Familiarize yourself with the generic name of your tablets, and tell your doctor or pharmacist if you think you're already using a similar product.

- P - Crosscheck the names of your medications and note whether the dose you've been given matches your **prescription**. If you notice any changes in your refills, let your pharmacist know. We're always happy to explain any changes to you - or help you rectify any mistakes.

With as many as 40,000 people dying from drug side effects every year[10], it's important to do everything you can to avoid becoming a statistic. Your garden needs compost to thrive, but using too much can smother and kill plants. Contaminated manure can devastate your carefully cultivated landscape. Likewise, taking your medications incorrectly or mixing them with an inappropriate substance may cause you more harm than good.

FOR EXCELLENT HEALTH DO THIS

Educating yourself about your medications and what to expect will help you get the treatment you need with minimum downside and maximum results..

In the next chapter, we'll go into some basic first aid principles. That way, you'll know exactly what to do if you suffer an unexpected side effect.

 Have you looked at your Workbook yet? If not, now's a great time. The activities that relate to chapter 2 are really helpful. Get yours at learnwellbooks.com/healthy

FIRST AID

Your First Step In Becoming An Everyday Hero

No Safety, Know Pain.
Know Safety, No Pain.

– Unknown

I'm used to dealing with medical problems at work, but there was one time when my expertise helped save my neighbor from being maimed or disfigured.

I was relaxing at home after a long day at work when my doorbell rang. I wasn't expecting anyone and when I went to answer, I was stunned to find my 17-year-old neighbor, Courtney, in obvious distress.

"You have to come help my brother!" she sobbed. "He's bleeding and it's bad."

She didn't wait to see if I was following her as she dashed back to her house. I quickly grabbed my first aid kit and hurried after her. Going into the kitchen, I found her younger brother, Andy, sitting on the floor, surrounded by little pieces of glass. He was bleeding heavily from a massive cut down his arm, and he was very pale.

"We were playing a game and Andy was running away from me. He tripped, and his arm went through the glass in the kitchen door," Courtney explained, as I examined Andy's injury.

"I don't think it's as bad as it looks," I reassured her. "Go fetch me a towel, so I can stop the bleeding."

Courtney quickly fetched a towel as I pulled on the gloves I kept in my first aid kit. When she came back, I pressed the towel on the wound.

"Have you called an ambulance?" I asked Courtney, keeping pressure on the cut to stem the flow of blood. I didn't want to worry her, but although I'd said the cut wasn't too bad, I could see it would need stitches.

"Not yet." Courtney shook her head as she got out her phone. Her hands were shaking as she tapped out 911.

"Everything's going to be okay," I told her after she finished the call. "Tell you what. Why don't you go make us all a drink? I'm sure you could do with one too."

I had an ulterior motive for sending Courtney away. She seemed even more stressed about her brother's accident than he was.

Their mom arrived home just as the ambulance pulled up. I passed the towel to her to allow her to support her son, and the two of them went off to hospital together.

Not long after that, Andy was proudly showing off his scar to me. "I tell everyone I got it fighting pirates!" he beamed, none the worse for his misadventure.

If I hadn't had training in first aid, things could have gone very differently. I believe that everyone should learn the basics of first aid because medical emergencies can happen at any time. According to a survey by the Red Cross, an incredible 59% of deaths from injuries could have been avoided if someone had administered first aid while waiting for emergency services to arrive[11].

WHAT TO DO IN A MEDICAL EMERGENCY

Stay Calm. Ideally, you would have received first aid training from a reputable provider. However, if you find yourself caught up in a medical emergency without that training, stay calm. If you panic, you are more likely to act from emotions, which may cause you to make decisions or take action which could make things worse. Do your best to approach the situation in a rational, logical fashion.

Assess. Assess the situation for risks, both to yourself and the casualty, as well as anyone else who may be involved. According to the Royal Society for the Prevention of Accidents (Rospa), seven people die every year in the UK trying to rescue their pets from drowning, only for the animal to find its own way to safety[12]. It's a natural, emotional reaction to want to save an animal in distress. Assessing the situation would mean that you would recognize that going after them would only endanger both of you. What makes these tragedies worse is that the animal is likely to be able to rescue itself.

Severity. Take a moment to assess the severity of the situation. It might be that the best thing to do is call an ambulance before tending to the patient. Alternatively, you may need to deal with them first and worry about getting help later. Your calm assessment of the situation will provide the best approach.

Prevent. Do your best to prevent possible transmission of diseases between you and the casualty, especially if blood is involved. If you can, wear latex or rubber gloves before tending to a wound - it's a good idea to keep a few pairs in your first aid kit.

Comfort. Comfort and reassure the casualty, which will help build trust with them. Be sympathetic towards them - they may be in shock or not fully understand what's happening.

First Aid. Give appropriate first aid (we'll go into some basics in a moment) and call 911 or your local emergency number as soon as you can.

Warning!. Never administer any medication if you're not sure of the use - you may be held legally liable for any adverse reactions.

Building your first aid kit

It's a good idea to put together a first aid kit or two, or even three! Keep one in your home, one in your car, and maybe a smaller one in your bag or purse.

You might like to include:

- A range of different size and shaped plasters
- Small, medium, and large sterile gauze dressings
- Sterile eye dressings
- Triangular bandages
- Crêpe rolled bandages
- Safety pins

FOR EXCELLENT HEALTH DO THIS

- Disposable sterile gloves
- Tweezers
- Scissors
- Alcohol-free cleansing wipes
- Sticky tape
- Digital thermometer
- Cream to treat skin rashes
- Insect bite/sting cream or spray
- Antiseptic cream
- Painkillers suitable for both adults and children
- Antihistamine cream or tablets
- Distilled water
- Eye wash and bath
- First aid manual or guide

Keep your first aid kit locked and well out of the reach of children in a cool, dry place. Regularly check your medicines to make sure they haven't gone out of date. Replace any items as soon as you use them.

FIRST AID FOR COMMON SITUATIONS

These are some of the most likely situations you might find yourself in and how to handle them.

DEALING WITH UNCONSCIOUS PATIENTS.

- If someone is unconscious, but still breathing with no obvious injuries that stop them being moved, particularly a spinal injury, place them in the recovery position until the emergency services arrive

The recovery position

- If you need to put someone in the recovery position, kneel on the floor next to them.
- Straighten their legs
- Place the arm nearest to you at a right angle to their body so their hand is pointing away from their body. Bend that arm at the elbow with their palm facing up. This will keep their hand out of the way when you roll them over.
- Pick up their other hand with their palm against yours. Turn any rings inward, so they don't scratch the face. Place the back of their hand on the opposite cheek, i.e. if it's their left hand place it against their right cheek or their right hand against their left cheek. You'll hold this hand in place as you roll them over. This hand will be between their face and the floor once you roll them over.
- Use your other arm to take hold of their furthest away knee and pull it up to bend their leg. The foot of this leg will end up flat on the floor.
- Gently pull this knee towards you, so they roll onto their side facing you. This should be quite straightforward, their body weight doing most of the work for you.

- Move the bent leg nearest to you in front of their body so it rests on the floor, supporting their body.
- Lightly raise their chin, tilting the head back slightly to open their airway and make it easy to breathe. Check there is nothing blocking the airway and remove any obstructions, such as food, if you can do this safely.
- Stay with the person until they have recovered or help arrives. Pay close attention to make sure they're still breathing normally.

If someone is unconscious and not breathing, call for emergency help and start CPR (cardiopulmonary resuscitation).

CPR ON ADULTS

If you've been trained in how to do CPR, give chest compressions with rescue breaths. If you haven't, just do hands-only CPR.

HANDS-ONLY CPR

Step One: If you need to carry out chest compressions, kneel next to the person and place the heel of your hand on the breastbone at the center of their chest. Put your other palm on top of that hand and interlock your fingers. Situate yourself with your shoulders directly above your hands.

Step Two: Use your body weight to press down hard on their chest. Don't be afraid to use all your strength. It's not uncommon for someone to suffer broken ribs as a consequence of CPR. It's better for them to recover from this later than not recover at all.

Step Three: Keep your hands on their chest as you release the compression.

Repeat this process at a pace of around 100-120 times a minute until help arrives, or for as long as you can keep it up.

CPR WITH RESCUE BREATHS

Step One: Follow the above process, but after every 30 compressions, give two rescue breaths:

Step Two: Gently tilt the patient's head back and lift the chin. Pinch their nose. Seal your mouth and blow steadily into their mouth for a second. Look to see that their chest rises. Do this twice.

Continue the cycle of 30 compressions and 2 rescue breaths until they start to recover or help arrives.

CPR ON CHILDREN

Children are more likely to have problems with their breathing than problems with their heart, so you should always combine compressions with rescue breaths.

CPR FOR CHILDREN AGED OVER 12 MONTHS

Step One: Open the child's airway by placing a hand on their forehead, gently tilting back their head and lifting their chin. Remove any obstructions from their mouth and nose.

FOR EXCELLENT HEALTH DO THIS

Step Two: Pinch the child's nose and seal your mouth over theirs. Blow steadily and firmly and look to see their chest rises. Give five rescue breaths.

Step Three: Place the heel of one hand in the center of the child's chest and push down about 2 inches. If you can't get to this depth with one hand, use two hands.

Step Four: Do 30 chest compressions at a rate of 100-120 a minute and then give two rescue breaths.

Continue this cycle until help arrives or the child starts to recover.

CPR ON INFANTS UNDER 12 MONTHS

Step One: Open the infant's airway by placing a hand on their forehead, gently tilting back their head and lifting their chin. Remove any obstructions from their mouth and nose.

Step Two: Pinch the infant's nose and seal your mouth over theirs. Blow steadily and firmly and look to see their chest rises. Give five rescue breaths.

Step Three: Place the heel of one hand on the center of the child's chest and push down about 1.5 inches. If you can't get to this depth with one hand, use two hands.

Step Four: Do 30 chest compressions at a rate of 100-120 a minute and then give two rescue breaths.

Continue this cycle until help arrives or the infant starts to recover.

One way of remembering this process is to consult DR ABC:

- Check for **D**anger
- Check to see if the patient **R**esponds.
- Open the **A**irways.
- Check they're **B**reathing.
- Check **C**irculation.

Treat as needed with CPR and/or the recovery position.

ANAPHYLAXIS

- Anaphylaxis or anaphylactic shock is a major allergic reaction, usually to insect stings or certain foods. They can happen very quickly, sometimes within seconds of coming into contact with an allergen. This may make it hard for the person to breathe because their tongue and throat may swell, blocking their airway.

- Call your emergency helpline (eg 911) immediately if you think someone is in anaphylactic shock.

- Check to see if they have any medication to treat their anaphylaxis, such as an adrenaline self-injector. You can help them administer their medication or give it yourself if you've been trained to do so.

- Make the patient comfortable. If they're conscious, sitting upright is probably the best position. Wait with the person until medical help arrives. If someone has had an adrenaline injection, they must be checked out by a medical professional as soon as possible.

SEVERE BLEEDING

If someone is badly bleeding, you should try to prevent further blood loss and minimize the impact of shock.

- Call emergency help and ask for an ambulance.
- If you have disposable gloves, put them on to reduce the chance of infection.
- If there is something embedded in the wound, do not press down on the item. Instead, press down firmly on either side and put padding around it before bandaging so you don't put any pressure on the object itself. Do not attempt to remove it - this could make the bleeding worse.
- If the wound is clean, apply and maintain pressure on the wound, using a clean pad or dressing if you have one. You can always use a makeshift dressing from items you have to hand such as a clean diaper or towel.
- Bandage the wound firmly.
- If blood seeps through the pad, continue to apply pressure to the wound until the bleeding stops and then place another pad over the top before bandaging it up.
- If the patient has severed a body part, such as a finger, put it in a plastic bag or wrap it in cling film. Then wrap this up in soft fabric and put it in a container with crushed ice. Do not let the body part touch the ice and don't wash it.

- Make sure the body part stays with the patient when they go to hospital.
- Unless a wound is minor, always seek medical assistance for bleeding.

BURNS AND SCALDS

If someone has a burn or scald:

- Cool the burn by placing the affected area under cool running water for at least 20 minutes.
- Call your emergency number or seek medical help if it's a serious burn.
- As you are cooling the burn, remove any clothing or jewelry unless it's stuck to the skin.
- Once the burn has cooled, cover it loosely with cling film or a clean, dry dressing made out of non-fluffy material.
- Do not put any creams, lotions, or sprays on the burn.
- If someone has suffered a chemical burn, make sure you put on protective gloves before treating the affected area. Remove any affected clothing and rinse the burn under cool running water for at least 20 minutes to remove any trace of the chemical.
- Depending on the chemical involved, there may be an antidote available for it.
- Take care to protect yourself from the chemical and call emergency help for immediate assistance.

CHOKING

If someone can speak, cry, cough or breathe, their airway is only partly blocked and they should be able to clear out the blockage themselves:

- Ask them to try to cough or spit out the object.

- Do not put your fingers in their mouth to try and remove the object if you can't see it because you may push it further down.

- If coughing or spitting doesn't work, hit them on the back to dislodge the object - a back blow.

If someone cannot speak, cry, cough, or breathe, they'll eventually fall unconscious. In this case, start back blows:

FOR AN ADULT OR CHILD AGED 12 MONTHS AND OVER

- Stand behind the choking person slightly to one side. Support their chest with one hand, placing the person so they're leaning slightly forward so when you dislodge the object it comes out of their mouth instead of going further down.

- Hit them up to five times between the shoulder blades with the heel of your hand (between your palm and wrist).

- Check if the blockage has gone.

- If not, perform up to five abdominal thrusts. (**NB - do not** perform abdominal thrusts on pregnant women or babies under 1 year old.)

- To do an abdominal thrust, stand behind the choking person.

- Place your arms around their waist and lean them forward.

- Make a first and put it just above the person's belly button.

- Put your other hand on top of your fist. Sharply pull inwards and upwards up to five times. If the item dislodges, you can stop doing the thrusts.

- If the airway is still blocked, call for emergency help and ask for an operator, saying it's for a choking person.

- Continuously repeat the cycle of 5 back blows and 5 abdominal thrusts until the object is dislodged or help arrives.

- Even if you are able to remove the obstruction, the affected individual should always be checked over by a medical professional in case of injury.

HEART ATTACK

Approximately 659,000 people die from heart disease every year in America alone - that's a quarter of all deaths[13].

If you think someone is suffering from a heart attack, call for emergency help and support them to get into a comfortable seated position, ideally on the floor with knees bent and head and shoulders supported. Symptoms to watch out for include:

- Chest pain, usually in the center or left side of the chest. It may feel like pressure, tightness, or squeezing around the heart.
- Pain in other parts of the body, as if the pain is traveling from the chest into the arms, jaw, neck, back or tummy.

If the patient is conscious:

- Give them a 300mg aspirin tablet and tell them to chew it slowly. (Unless aspirin is contraindicated, e.g. if the individual is under 16 or has an allergy to aspirin.)[14]
- If the patient is on medication for angina, support them to take it.
- Monitor vital signs until help arrives.
- If the patient becomes unconscious, make sure their airway is open, check their breathing and start CPR if you feel it necessary.
- Call for emergency help again and tell them that the person is in cardiac arrest/their heart has stopped.

STROKE

If someone has suffered a stroke, call for emergency assistance and act FAST:

Face - see if their face has dropped on one side. Alternatively, they may not be able to smile, or you may notice drooping in the mouth or eye.

Arms - they may not be able to lift both their arms or keep them up due to weakness or numbness in one of their arms.

Speech - their speech may become slurred or garbled, if they are able to talk at all.

Time - time to call your local emergency number (eg 911) if someone is displaying any of these signs or symptoms.

If someone experienced any of these symptoms, but these have now passed, you should still call for help because they may have suffered a mini-stroke.

ALTERNATIVE FIRST AID REMEDIES

You may be able to treat some problems using home remedies. Be aware that the use of some of these may be controversial or have limited scientific evidence for their efficacy. They are not a replacement for medications. Try to limit their use to when you don't have access to conventional drugs. Nevertheless, some of my customers swear by turmeric to treat their pain and inflammation[15]. (Turmeric contains curcumin and other chemicals which are known to combat inflammation.) Others like drinking mint tea for an upset stomach.[16] (Research has found that the compounds in peppermint can activate an anti-pain channel in the colon. This may lower pain caused by eating spicy foods.)

STOMACH ULCERS

There is evidence that bananas are a natural treatment for stomach ulcers[17]. The best way to take them is to crush them with honey, add liquid (water or milk) and drink three times a day. In addition, avoid acidic foods, such as citrus fruits, alcohol, and cigarettes.

Some like to take baking powder to relieve the symptoms of stomach ulcers, but you should be aware that although it can provide temporary relief, over time, it will make things worse[18].

HEADACHES

Caffeine has been demonstrated to relieve headaches[19]. You can take this in the form of coffee, kolanut, bitter kola, etc.

The problem with caffeine is that it can also cause headaches! Your body can adjust to its effects if you're consuming it regularly so when you don't have any caffeine in your system, which can cause withdrawal symptoms, which includes - you guessed it - headaches.

Caffeine can also cause what's known as a rebound headache. This is what you get if you take a painkiller too often. When its effect wears off, the pain returns only worse. If you've been combining caffeine with more conventional pain killers, this type of headache is more likely.

COLDS AND FLU

We all know there's no cure for the common cold other than time and bed rest with plenty of fluids. However, many people like to drink honey, lemon, and ginger in an attempt to speed the healing process, and this may not be as far-fetched as you'd think. Honey is known to soothe the throat[20], while lemon is filled with vitamin C and has antibacterial properties[21]. Ginger has many health benefits[22] - as well as being good for colds and flu, it can also help combat nausea, especially during pregnancy.

I could write an entire book about first aid. Maybe one day I will. But for now, this chapter should have given you enough of an overview so that you can provide vital help as soon as you notice a health problem. In some situations, a patient's condition can deteriorate rapidly without that immediate assistance. Your intervention could be what stabilizes them until professional help arrives.

You could, quite literally, save a life.

In the next chapter, we're going to examine two of the most important organs and you'll learn how to take care of them.

YOUR KIDNEY AND LIVER

How You Can Protect These Two Little Heroes

Is life worth living? It all depends upon the liver.

– William James

"Have you got anything stronger for a headache?" The young woman shook a bottle of acetaminophen (paracetamol) at me. "My head's been killing me for days, but I haven't got time to go back to the doctor's. I'm already behind on work thanks to an infected insect bite. Just my luck - the antibiotics cleared up the infection, but now I feel even worse!"

"Hmmm," I gazed critically at the woman, taking in the yellow tinge to her eyes. She looked gaunt, as though chronic pain was taking its toll on her health. "Is it just a headache?"

"Well, I feel tired and nauseous all the time, and I can't bear the thought of food, but I put that down to the headache."

"And you say you've just had antibiotics?"

"That's right," She nodded.

"I don't want to alarm you, but I think you should go straight to the emergency room and get your bloods checked," I said. "By the look of you, you might have jaundice. It can sometimes happen after certain antibiotics, but it's really rare. Still, I think you should be on the safe side and get yourself tested."

"I will." She hurried out of the pharmacy and I didn't see her until a few months later. The woman who walked up to my counter looked completely different. Her skin had lost its yellow pallor and her cheeks had filled out, making her look healthier. She seemed much happier in herself.

"I wanted to come back to thank you," she said. "I took your advice and got some blood tests. It took a while to get a proper diagnosis, but it turned out that I had a reaction to the antibiotics. They called it a drug-induced liver injury. Fortunately, we caught it and it didn't get too serious. The doctors tell me I'm going to have to take it easy for a while yet, but if it wasn't for you, it could have been so much worse. I've also got an appointment to get myself checked out for any other drug allergies. Just to make sure the same thing doesn't happen again."

The liver and kidney are the two most important organs when it comes to how your body processes any medications. The liver controls how your body metabolizes a drug, while the kidney excretes unwanted materials. If either organ fails to function effectively, this can lead to a toxic build-up of the drug or its metabolites, which can cause irreparable damage if left untreated.

The first pass effect or first-pass metabolism is the process whereby the concentration of a drug is heavily reduced before it is circulated around the body after being swallowed. The drug is absorbed by the digestive system, going to the hepatic portal system, where the portal vein takes it to the liver. The liver then metabolizes the drug, sometimes so much so that very little of the active drug leaves the liver to travel through the circulatory system. This 'first pass' through the liver means that the bioavailability of the drug may be drastically reduced.

Meanwhile, the kidneys play a major role in removing drugs from the body. Most drugs are usually passed out of the body in urine. This is particularly the case with water-soluble ones and their metabolites, Some are eliminated by excretion in the bile. The acidity of urine can be affected by diet, drugs, and kidney disorders, which can impact on the rate at which kidneys can excrete drugs. Kidney function can also be affected by the amount of urine flow, the quality of blood flow through the kidneys and the condition of the kidneys themselves.

As such, if there's a problem with either or both of these organs, the way drugs affect your body can be heavily affected. Your doctor may need to increase or reduce your dosage to achieve the required response, or try a different drug altogether. Moreover, damage to these organs can severely reduce your quality of life.

THE CAUSES OF KIDNEY AND LIVER FAILURES

There are a number of different reasons why you might develop problems with your kidney and/or liver.

> **Medications.** One of the most common causes of liver failure is an overdose of acetaminophen, either accidentally or intentionally. This may also result in kidney failure. In the United States, over 100,000 cases of acetaminophen overdose occur every year[23]. In the United Kingdom, it is the number one cause of medication overdose[24]. It is the most common cause of poisonings in young children, so make sure you keep any medications locked away[25]. Other medications that carry a risk of liver or kidney damage include statins, NSAIDS, antibiotics and some arthritis drugs. You should also be aware that aspirin, ibuprofen, and naproxen sodium may lead to toxic liver disease if you take too many or take them with alcohol.
>
> **Infections and medical conditions.** Hepatitis is one of the biggest causes of liver failure, but there are other

conditions which may also cause problems, including diabetes and genetic conditions such as hemochromatosis and Wilson's disease

Diet. Most of us know that too much alcohol can negatively impact your liver, but that's not the only thing which can damage your organs. Research by the Nurses' Health Society found that drinking several diet sodas a day could damage your kidneys. Compared with women who didn't drink diet soda, soda-drinking women experienced 30% lower kidney function over 20 years[26]. Excess salt can also damage your kidneys[27] and liver[28]. With these vital organs, prevention is much better than the cure, so try to reduce your consumption of food and drinks known to affect your liver and kidney.

Accidents. Your organs can be damaged through no fault of your own, like if you're involved in a car crash or suffer trauma from a knife or gunshot wound.

THE SYMPTOMS OF LIVER AND KIDNEY FAILURE

If your liver or kidney stop working, the impact can be life-threatening, so it's important to be aware of the signs of liver or kidney failure. Early intervention is essential to prevent further damage. While the symptoms outlined below don't always mean a problem with your organs, if you notice them, it's always best to get yourself assessed because they could be the sign of something serious.

Fluid retention. 50% of people with cirrhosis (scarring) of the liver suffer from fluid retention[29]. This can lead to an accumulation of fluid in the abdomen or swelling in the legs and ankles. This is the most common sign of liver damage and may also indicate kidney damage.

Jaundice. One of the liver's functions is to filter out bilirubin, a yellow-colored bile pigment. If the liver is damaged, bilirubin can build up. This makes the skin and eyes look yellowish. You may suffer from itchy skin if you have jaundice. Dry, itchy skin can also be a sign of the mineral and bone disease which frequently occurs with advanced kidney disease.

Nausea/Loss of appetite. If your liver and/or kidneys aren't filtering out toxins properly, they build up in your bloodstream, which can make you feel nauseous or even vomit. As the damage gets worse, you may also experience a loss of appetite, diarrhea, abdominal pain and problems with digestion.

Fatigue and lethargy. A decline in kidney function can result in toxins and impurities in the blood, making you feel tired and weak. In addition, you may suffer from insomnia due to these toxins. Anemia is another side effect of kidney disease, which may also make you feel fatigued.

Pale stools. Yes, we're going to talk about poo for a moment. Much as you may not like examining your stools, they can give us essential information about your current state of health. Normal stools are dark because of the bile salts released by the liver. If you notice your stools are a lighter color, it could be a sign of liver damage. Alternatively, your stools may look black or tarry due to blood going through the digestive system. Conversely, your urine may look darker because of the build up of bilirubin. Damage to the kidneys may give you the urge to urinate more often, and you may see blood in your urine due to damage to the kidney's filters. If you ever vomit blood or see blood in your stool or urine, seek medical attention immediately.

Bruising. When liver function is impaired, it can't produce the right level of clotting proteins, making you more prone to bruising and bleeding. Bruising can also be a sign of other disorders (or simply that you've bumped into something!). On its own, bruising may not be a sign of liver damage.

MAINTAINING GOOD KIDNEY AND LIVER HEALTH

As with all health problems, there's a lot you can do to lower your risk of developing kidney or liver disease. You keep a vegetable garden weed free and well fertilized, so you can enjoy delicious, fresh food. Likewise, looking after your body with the right nutrients and habits can help you stay healthy for longer.

Stay hydrated. Drinking 6-8 glasses of water a day will help keep you hydrated and help your liver and kidneys efficiently flush out toxins.

Eat healthily. Most kidney problems are the consequence of other medical conditions such as high blood pressure, diabetes, and cardiovascular disease. Obesity is a known factor in developing these conditions, so eating a healthy diet will help control your weight, avoid developing diabetes and keep your blood pressure down. Reducing your salt intake can also help, as will cutting back on (or cutting out!) alcohol.

Exercise. Regular physical activity can help keep you fit, preventing weight gain and keeping your blood pressure down. Be careful about starting any new exercise regime, especially if you're new to working out. Not exercising or overdoing it can both cause problems. Consult a health or fitness professional before embarking on a new fitness program.

Be careful with supplements and herbal remedies. There is evidence that some supplements can support liver and kidney health. For example, milk thistle may have a positive impact on liver function[30]. However, if you have kidney disease, supplements and herbal remedies can cause even more damage. Some herbal supplements, such as juniper berries, or parsley capsules, are diuretic and can be harmful if you have kidney problems. Many herbal supplements can interfere with prescription drugs. They should never be taken without consulting your doctor first. Examples include St. John's Wort, echinacea, ginkgo, garlic, ginger, ginseng, and blue cohosh. Some herbal supplements are very dangerous for patients with kidney disease and should be completely avoided. These include barberry, java tea leaf, licorice root, nettle, pennyroyal and Oregon grape root. If you suffer from any liver or kidney problems, **always** consult a medical professional first. Just because something's natural doesn't mean it can't harm you.

FOR EXCELLENT HEALTH DO THIS

Quit smoking or vaping. We all know that smoking severely damages the body. One of the side effects is damage to the blood vessels, which means less flow of blood to the kidneys. In turn, inadequate blood flow means reduced kidney function. Smoking also increases the risk of cancer and high blood pressure. While you might think you're improving things by vaping instead of smoking, there are still a lot of chemicals in the solution, which also contains nicotine, which is highly addictive.

Practice safe sex. Hepatitis is a major cause of liver failure. Be sure to practice safe sex to reduce your chances of contracting the virus (or any other sexually transmitted infection).

Use over-the-counter medications responsibly. Common non-prescription pills such as ibuprofen and naproxen can damage your kidneys if taken regularly over a prolonged period. If you're using them to treat chronic pain, discuss alternatives with your doctor. They may want to monitor your kidney function or look at different ways of dealing with your pain. **Never** take paracetamol if you know you have severe liver problems.

Your liver and kidney are two of the most important organs when it comes to metabolizing medications. Taking care of your liver and kidney can also improve your overall health - a healthy liver and kidney means a healthy body! Eat nutritious food, get regular, appropriate exercise, and be aware of the symptoms. It'll give you a great chance of enjoying good liver and kidney function for a lifetime.

In the next chapter, we're going to turn our attention to the mind and some common mental health problems you should watch out for.

5

MENTAL AND NEUROLOGICAL DISORDERS

Your Mind Does Matter

What mental health needs is more sunlight, more candor, and more unashamed conversation.

– Glenn Close

We all have our good and bad days. Sometimes I wonder whether what I do really makes any difference. Then I'll have a conversation with one customer which instantly restores the belief in my practice.

It was a normal day at work. A man came up to my counter to fill a prescription for a course of antibiotics. When he saw me, his face lit up.

"It's so lovely to see you again," he beamed. "But I bet you don't remember me?"

"I'm sorry." I shook my head. "You do look familiar, but I can't say how I know you."

"You really helped my daughter when she was going through a rough time," he told me. "She'd been prescribed some antidepressants, but she really didn't want to take them. She was worried about the side effects and felt that the pills weren't really going to help."

"Oh, I think I remember now," I said. "Her name's Jenny, right?"

"That's right."

Jenny had been prescribed some high dose antidepressants. At the time, I didn't want to pry but it was clear that she was going through a really rough time.

"How's she doing now?"

"She's getting married, would you believe?" The proud father pulled out his phone and started showing me some photos of his daughter and her fiancé . "She's in a really good place. You helped her understand the difference medication could make to her, but you were also honest about the side effects and what they couldn't do for her. You helped her decide to start taking the pills. They did a lot to help her recovery. You could say that without your kind words, there's no way she'd be able to rebuild her life."

I cannot express how much it meant to me to hear that. As a pharmacist, I don't always see the impact of my work but I'll never forget the gratitude on that man's face as he told me about his daughter's journey.

We still have a lot to learn about mental illness. There's debate over the importance of nature or nature. People with the same condition may not experience the same symptoms. treatment will vary depending on personal circumstance. Left untreated, mental illness can cause all sorts of problems. It can make it hard to find and keep a job. You may have problems with building and maintaining relationships. Mental illness may even lead to violence or, tragically, suicide.

Symptoms like anxiety, anger, mood swings, and depression can be a normal response to life, but there's a point at which they become problematic. It's important to know when you or someone you love may be experiencing mental health problems. That way you can seek help before things get worse.

I'd also like you to know that regardless of your struggles, you are never alone. Readers of this book, along with those reading the LearnWell books on mental health, are in the LearnWell Community. Social support is one of the best complementary treatments for mental

health challenges. I suggest joining and being a part of something uplifting.

SOME OF THE MOST COMMON MENTAL HEALTH DISORDERS

Anxiety is the brain's way of dealing with stress and letting you know about possible danger. Anxiety can have many causes - money problems, an important test, or facing a difficult decision. It's natural to feel anxious in these sorts of circumstances, but anxiety disorders are different. They are a type of mental illness which causes you to feel constantly anxious and afraid. This can make you avoid triggering situations such as work, school, and social gatherings. Common anxiety disorders include:

- Generalized anxiety disorder, when you feel excessive amounts of worry or tension without reason
- Panic disorder, which makes you feel a sudden intense fear bringing on a panic attack
- Social anxiety disorder, which makes you feel stressed about everyday social situations.
- Some medications or illegal drugs can trigger symptoms of anxiety. Researchers still haven't pinpointed the exact cause of anxiety disorders. There are a number of factors which could bring it on. These included genetics, brain chemistry, or environmental stress. Fortunately, there are a number of treatments available for anxiety disorder.

Bipolar disorder is a mental health condition characterized by extreme mood swings. Sufferers go from emotional highs (mania or hypomania) to extreme lows (depression). When someone with bipolar disorder is depressed, they may find it difficult to do anything. They may feel overwhelmed by feelings of misery and hopelessness. When they are experiencing a manic phase, they feel filled with energy. It's as though anything is possible. Bipolar disorder is a lifelong condition, but it can be managed. The best approach is to follow a treatment plan put together with a medical team. It is most commonly treated with a combination of medication and psychotherapy. The cause of bipolar disorder is unknown, although it is believed that genetics and biological differences play a part. People with bipolar disorder may not always realize how much their emotional instability impacts on their life and those around them. This means they don't always seek treatment. Bipolar disorder does not improve without support. If you have any symptoms of depression or mania, consult your doctor or mental health professional to see if you might benefit from treatment to control your symptoms.

Schizophrenia is a mental health condition which usually starts showing symptoms in late adolescence or early adulthood. It is relatively uncommon, affecting approximately 0.25%-0.64% of people in the United States[31]. It is a lifelong condition, but can be managed with medication. It impacts on different people in different ways. Common symptoms include confused speech, a lack of facial or emotional expression,

Mental and Neurological Disorders

difficulty getting motivated, problems concentrating and psychosis, including delusions or hallucinations. Many people with schizophrenia don't realize they are unwell. Delusions and hallucinations can seem incredibly realistic to the person experiencing them. This can make it difficult for them to take medication. They may be afraid of the side effects or think it's going to harm them. Schizophrenia is usually caused by genetics, a chemical imbalance in the brain, and environmental factors. There is also evidence to suggest that cannabis can trigger schizophrenia if someone is susceptible[32]. Treatment for schizophrenia needs to be tailored to the individual. It may include antipsychotic drugs, counseling, or working with the family and education services to provide support along with medication.

Post traumatic stress disorder or PTSD is a mental health disorder caused by experiencing or witnessing a terrifying event. Symptoms may include flashbacks, nightmares, thoughts about the event, negative changes in thinking or mood, and severe anxiety. These symptoms may appear within a month of the event. However, they may not appear until years later. They may vary over time or from person to person. They can cause serious problems in social or work situations, and impact on someone's ability to perform their daily tasks. Discuss the possibility of PTSD with your doctor or a mental health professional:

- If you're having troubling thoughts or feelings about a traumatic event for over a month

- If these thoughts are interfering with your ability to function
- If you're finding it hard to get your life under control

Early treatment can help prevent your symptoms from worsening.

It is unclear why some people develop PTSD after a traumatic event and others don't. PTSD can also increase your chances of developing other mental health problems. These include depression, anxiety, drug or alcohol abuse, eating disorders, or suicidal tendencies.

If you've experienced a traumatic event, it's important to get help. This could help prevent normal stress reactions from developing into PTSD. There are a number of therapies for PTSD, which include EMDR (Eye Movement Desensitization and Reprocessing) or hypnosis.

WHAT TO AVOID IF YOU'RE TAKING MEDICATION FOR YOUR MENTAL ILLNESS

There is no shame involved in getting help for your mental illness. Medications can be literal lifesavers in these circumstances. However, you should be aware of some contraindications so you don't accidentally cause yourself more harm.

- If you're on lithium, avoid taking Advil/ibuprofen or other NSAIDS to treat pain. When combined, NSAIDs can increase the lithium levels in the blood. This puts you more at risk for adverse side effects like confusion, tremors, slurred speech, or vomiting.

Mental and Neurological Disorders

- If you are taking antidepressants like phenelzine, avoid cheese. Believe it or not, this could kill you! The tyramine in aged cheese can react with phenelzine to increase your blood pressure, causing a hypertensive crisis.

- If you have a mental health illness, alcohol is best avoided. Alcohol causes chemical changes in the brain, negatively impacting your mood. It can affect personal relationships. It makes it harder for you to sleep. It increases your chances of developing depression or anxiety. Drinking alcohol when you are on certain medications (such as benzodiazepines) can be dangerous. It can significantly slow down your breathing. Check with your pharmacist to see if you can drink while you're on your medication.

- Marijuana is the most popular illicit drug across the world[33]. Many people think it's perfectly safe. However, if you're taking psychiatric medications, marijuana can make depression and anxiety worse. In recent years, marijuana has become stronger and is often mixed with other substances. This means that even short-term use may cause hallucinations, paranoia and anxiety.

- Herbal supplements aren't subject to the same regulation as traditional medicine. Studies show mixed results about their efficacy and safety. If you are considering using herbal supplements to treat your mental health, be aware it's not a replacement for getting help from a qualified healthcare provider. For example, St. John's Wort is a popular herbal supplement taken for depression. When combined with antidepressants it can cause serotonin toxicity. This results in shivering, diarrhea, muscle rigidity, fever, and seizures.

Valerian root is often taken for anxiety or insomnia, but there is scant evidence for its effectiveness. Care should be exercised if you're taking Valerian root along with other medications which cause sleepiness or drowsiness.

NEUROLOGICAL CONDITIONS

Neurological conditions are not the same as mental health disorders. However, they are disorders of the nervous system, and can sometimes cause similar symptoms to mental health disorders. We're going to go into some of the most common neurological disorders so you're aware of them. Understanding these things is helpful should you ever detect that you have your own experience with them. Also, it allows for much greater empathy when people around you exhibit the characteristics of these conditions. You may find that you're the only one that understands them.

Parkinson's disease is a progressive nervous disorder that affects your movement. It has a slow onset, usually starting with a very slight tremor in the hand. While tremors are the most common symptom, it may also cause stiffness or a slowing of movement. In the early stages, your face may become less expressive, your arms may stop swinging when you walk, or your speech may become slurred. Symptoms worsen as the condition progresses. If you have any symptoms associated with Parkinson's, consult a medical professional to rule out other potential causes. When someone has Parkinson's disease, neurons in the brain slowly break down or die. Many of the symptoms result from the loss of neurons which produce dopamine.

Mental and Neurological Disorders

When dopamine levels fall, it causes abnormal brain activity. This causes the impaired movement and other symptoms associated with Parkinson's. The condition may also cause cognitive problems, including dementia, in the later stages. Sufferers may develop depression or other emotional changes, such as anxiety. They may also experience problems chewing and swallowing, insomnia, incontinence, or constipation. The cause of Parkinson's is unknown, but it could be due to genetics, and environmental triggers. You are more at risk of developing Parkinson's as you get older. Having a close relative with the condition also increases your chances. Men are more likely to develop Parkinson's than women. There is currently no cure for Parkinson's, but medications can help relieve the symptoms. In some instances, your doctor might suggest surgery to improve symptoms.

Epilepsy is a neurological disorder which involves abnormal brain activity. This can cause seizures, unusual behavior, or loss of awareness. Symptoms can vary widely between individuals. Some people just stare blankly for a brief period during a seizure, while others find their arms and legs twitching. Other associated symptoms include:

- Temporary confusion
- An uncontrollable jerking of the arms and legs
- Loss of consciousness
- Psychological problems such as fear, anxiety, or deja vu.

Having a seizure doesn't mean you have epilepsy. You need to have had at least two seizures at least 24 hours apart without an identified trigger to be diagnosed with the condition.

There are medications available to treat epilepsy. Surgery is also an option for some. Some people need treatment for life to control their seizures, while others find they eventually go away.

You should seek immediate medical assistance if:

- The seizure lasts more than five minutes
- Breathing or consciousness doesn't come back after the end of the seizure
- You have an immediate second seizure;
- You have a fever
- You're pregnant
- You have diabetes
- You suffered an injury during the seizure
- You're taking anti-seizure medication but you still have a seizure.

You should also consult a medical professional if you have a seizure for the first time.

In about half of epilepsy sufferers, there is no identifiable cause. For the other half, a number of factors could be at play. These include genetics, head trauma, brain abnormalities, infections, prenatal injury, and developmental disorders such as autism. People with epilepsy are more likely to suffer from mental health problems such as depression, anxiety, and suicidal thoughts and behaviors. These may arise due to the problems associated with

Mental and Neurological Disorders

dealing with the condition. They may also be side effects from the medication.

Multiple sclerosis (MS) is a potentially disabling disease of the brain and central nervous system. The immune system attacks the myelin, a protective sheath covering the nerve fibers. This makes it difficult for the brain to communicate with the rest of the body. Over time, the condition can cause deterioration of the nerves or even permanent damage.

The signs and symptoms of MS differ widely from person to person. It depends on how much nerve damage has been done and which nerves have been affected. Some people eventually lose the ability to walk. There may also be long periods of time where no new symptoms develop. Other symptoms can include numbness or weakness in the limbs, tremors, electric-shock sensations, problems with vision, slurred speech, fatigue, and dizziness.

There is no known cure for MS. However, there are treatments which can speed recovery from attacks, slow the progress of the disease and control symptoms. For most people, the disease follows a cycle of relapse and remission, which vary in length. You should consult a doctor if you experience any of the symptoms of MS without explanation.

The cause of MS is unknown. Age is a risk factor, with people most likely to develop it during 20 and 40 years of age. Women are more likely than men to develop relapsing-remitting MS. If a close family member has had

MS, you are at increased risk of developing the disorder. You are also more likely to develop it following certain infections, such as Epstein-Barr.

We need to end the stigma surrounding mental health disorders. It shouldn't be a source of shame to have a brain which is functioning in a different way to others'. There are a lot of treatments available to improve the symptoms of mental health problems, usually a combination of medication and psychotherapy. It's a very personal journey, so always work with a healthcare professional to come up with the right treatment plan.

Neurological disorders are a result of problems with the brain, but they are distinct to mental health disorders. There is no cure for many neurological disorders, but there are treatments to alleviate symptoms. The sooner you start treatment, the better. If you suspect you may be suffering from a neurological condition, seek help immediately.

In the next chapter, we'll be moving from the brain down to the heart to look at what you can do to keep your heart healthy.

 Your Workbook includes a mental health tracker as well. It will accompany you for a week, month, year or however long you feel like using it. Open your Journal now to take a look Or, grab your copy at learnwellbooks.com/healthy

6

YOUR HEART

Tips For A Tip Top Ticker

The worst time to have a cardiac arrest is during a game of charades.

– Demetri Martin

"It's for my husband," the woman explained, passing me a prescription for beta-blockers. She couldn't have been much older than thirty, but worry lines were already marking her face. "He just went for a regular check-up and they told him his blood pressure was too high. They said it was 160 over 100 - is that high?"

"It is." I nodded as I checked the details of the script. Beta-blockers lower your blood pressure by slowing down your heart rate. With a blood pressure as high as the woman's husband, it was important he got it back under control.

She sighed. "I kept telling him not to put so much salt on his fries and to cut back on the number of burgers he ate. It's not like he couldn't do with losing a few pounds. But he only laughed and said he was too young to worry about things like that. I guess he's not laughing now, is he?"

"Hopefully these will sort him out." I went and got the beta-blockers and the woman left the store.

Usually, I see people on a reasonably regular basis as they come back to get refills on their medication. Obviously, sometimes they go to other pharmacies, but even so, I generally tend to get to know the ones who have chronic conditions like hypertension. However, I didn't see that woman again until around a year later. This time, she was carrying a prescription for beta-blockers, ACE inhibitors, angiotensin receptor blockers, calcium-channel blockers and diuretics - the full works! Clearly something had gone very wrong with her husband's health.

I said nothing as I handed over a bag filled with pills, but obviously, the expression on my face must have spoken volumes.

"He had a stroke," the woman explained without me having to ask. "The silly man stopped taking his pills, saying they made him feel like a zombie. He brushed it off when he started feeling nauseous all the time, just changed the place he went for burgers in case it was food poisoning. But then his vision went all blurry and he started vomiting whenever he moved. I rushed him to emergency and the nurse there said she'd never seen blood pressure so high. It was off the charts! They took him straight to intensive care where they told me he'd had three brain hemorrhages due to high blood pressure. His kidney function was down to 60% as well because he was too stubborn to take his pills. They've finally released him from hospital, but he's going to have to take these every day if he wants to stay alive. And this time, I'm going to stand over him and make sure he takes them!" She rattled the bag at me as she walked out of the pharmacy.

Her husband was lucky to have survived. Hypertension, or high blood pressure, is often known as the silent killer because sometimes the only symptom is sudden death!

The cardiovascular system is crucial to good health. The heart pumps blood around the body, taking oxygen everywhere it's needed. If there's a problem anywhere in that system, it can lead to stroke or heart attack. Heart disease is the leading cause of death in the US. One in four people die from heart disease[34]. Taking good care of your heart is one of the most important things you can do for a long and healthy life.

HYPERTENSION

Blood pressure is the pressure of blood in your arteries. The arteries carry blood from your heart to the brain and throughout your body. If you are suffering from hypertension, your heart has to work harder to pump blood around your body. It can then result in heart and circulatory diseases. It can also cause kidney or heart failure, sight problems, or vascular dementia. It's normal for your blood pressure to vary during the day and go up when you're exercising. But if your blood pressure is consistently high even when resting, it requires your immediate attention.

There isn't always an identifiable cause for high blood pressure. For most people, their diet, lifestyle or other medical conditions results in high blood pressure. Drinking too much alcohol, smoking, obesity, not enough exercise, or eating too much salt all increase your risk. In some instances, secondary hypertension can be caused by another condition, such as an abnormal production of hormones from the adrenal glands. Treating the underlying condition should see the blood pressure return to normal. Some medicines such as oral contraceptives and some over-the-counter drugs and herbal remedies can raise your blood pressure. Make sure to ask your doctor or pharmacist if you have any concerns about the side effects of your medication.

Since hypertension is usually symptomless, the only way to know if you have it is to check your blood pressure. You can buy your own monitor to check your blood pressure or get your doctor or nurse to measure it. The result will be written as two numbers. The first is when your blood pressure is at its highest (systolic pressure). The second is when it's at its lowest (diastolic pressure).

- Low blood pressure has a systolic of under 90 mmHg and diastolic of under 60 mHg

- Normal blood pressure has a systolic of under 140 mmHg and diastolic of under 90 mmHg

- High blood pressure has a systolic of 140-180 mmHg and a diastolic of 90-110 mmHg

- Severe high blood pressure has a systolic of over 180 mmHg and a diastolic of over 110 mmHg.

If your blood pressure is consistently high, you will be offered medication to try to lower it. The most common are ACE inhibitors, angiotensin receptor blockers (ARBs), calcium-channel blockers, diuretics, alpha-blockers and beta-blockers. Most people will need to take more than one type of medicine to lower blood pressure. Research suggests that a combination of two or more drugs is more effective than just one[35].

ISCHEMIC (UH-SKEE-MUHK) HEART DISEASE

Ischemia is a condition which means the blood flow is reduced or restricted in a certain part of the body. Cardiac ischemia is the term for when the blood flow to the heart muscle is decreased. Ischemic heart disease is when narrowed heart arteries mean less blood and oxygen reaches the heart muscle, which can eventually result in a heart attack.

Ischemia can often cause angina pectoris, chest pain or discomfort. Many people have ischemic episodes without realizing. This is what's called silent ischemia. Just as with hypertension, the first symptom can be serious, like a sudden heart attack.

FOR EXCELLENT HEALTH DO THIS

You are at increased risk of suffering from ischemic heart disease if:

- You are male and over 45 or female and over 55. The difference between the sexes is due to the influence of hormones on the blood vessels.

- You smoke. This is one of the most common risk factors yet one of the most preventable.

- You suffer from hypertension.

- You have high levels of LDL cholesterol, the 'bad' cholesterol. Conversely, high levels of HDL cholesterol, the 'good' type, can protect against heart disease.

- You have diabetes.

- You have a family history of heart disease at a young age (under 55 in men or under 65 in women).

- You live a sedentary life.

- You are obese. Even losing just a little weight can really help your cardiovascular system.

- You are under stress or feel anxious.

- You take illegal drugs such as cocaine or amphetamines. These can change how the arteries work and cause a vascular spasm, stopping blood flow. Cocaine is a relatively common cause of heart attacks among the young[36].

- You are pregnant and develop preeclampsia or an autoimmune disease.

Initially, lifestyle changes are the best treatment for stable ischemic heart disease. We'll dig into these in more depth later in this chapter. You may find yourself prescribed antiplatelet therapy or dual antiplatelet therapy which improve arterial circulation. Some patients do well with beta-blockers, or calcium-channel blockers. If improving your lifestyle and taking your medications doesn't have a big enough impact, surgery may be advised.

STROKE

In the USA, 1 in 6 deaths from cardiovascular disease are due to a stroke. Every 36 seconds, someone in the States suffers a stroke. Almost 800,000 people have a stroke every year[37]. It can happen to anyone at any time, so it's important to know how to identify the symptoms of a stroke and act FAST:

>**Facial weakness -** notice if the person can smile or their mouth or eyes are drooping.
>
>**Arm weakness -** check if the person can raise both their arms.
>
>**Speech problems -** can the person speak clearly and do they understand you?
>
>**Time to call for emergency help** if you spot any of these signs. This will give the stroke sufferer the best chance of surviving.

While these are the main signs of a stroke, other symptoms which should also be considered, such as:

- A sudden sensation of weakness or numbness down one side of the body.
- Trouble finding words or forming a coherent sentence.
- Blurred vision or loss of sight in one or both eyes
- Sudden memory loss, confusion, or dizziness.
- A sudden, powerful headache.

While anyone may suffer a stroke, some things that increase your risk are:

Age. As we grow olders, the arteries naturally narrow and harden. They may become clogged with fatty material (atherosclerosis).

Some medical conditions. High blood pressure, diabetes, atrial fibrillation, and high cholesterol increase your risk of a stroke.

Lifestyle. Smoking, drinking too much alcohol, obesity and an unhealthy diet can damage your blood vessels. They can also increase your blood pressure and make your blood more likely to clot.

Family history. If a close family member has a stroke, you are more at risk.

Ethnicity. Strokes occur more often in people who are black or South Asian.

Sex. Women have some sex-specific risk factors. These include being pregnant or taking the combined contraceptive pill.

Sickle cell disease. This is an inherited condition which affects the red blood cells.

Migraines. While migraines have not been proven to cause strokes, if you suffer from migraines with an aura (classic migraine), you are at an elevated risk of stroke.

There are a number of different treatments available for ischemic strokes. Some medications need to be taken as soon as possible and then only for a short while. Others will be given after the stroke has been treated and may be required as a long term course.

Thrombolysis is injections of alteplase which dissolves blood clots and restores the blood flow to the brain. This is most effective if given within 4.5 hours of the onset of a stroke. It is unclear whether it has any benefit after this time. A brain scan needs to be carried out to confirm that the patient has suffered an ischemic stroke before giving alteplase. If they are actually experiencing a hemorrhagic stroke, it will make the stroke worse.

Thrombectomy is an emergency procedure which removes blood clots to restore blood flow to the brain. This is only effective if the stroke has been caused by a blood clot in a large artery in the brain.

Aspirin is a painkiller and antiplatelet which can help treat strokes. However, many people shouldn't take aspirin, since it could make other conditions worse. These include gout or a blood clotting problem. Other antiplatelet medications are available.

Anticoagulants may lower the risk of future blood clots. They change the chemical composition of blood to stop clots forming. These are available in pill form, e.g. warfarin, or as injections, i.e. heparins.

Blood pressure medications may be offered to bring down your blood pressure if this is a contributing factor.

Statins may be advised if your cholesterol is too high.

Carotid endarterectomy is a surgical procedure which opens up the carotid artery to remove the fatty deposits which limit the flow of blood to the brain.

ATHEROSCLEROSIS

Atherosclerosis is the result of fatty deposits building up inside your arteries, making them harder and narrower. This increases the chances of blocks. We all suffer from thicker, less flexible arteries as we age, but atherosclerosis can speed this process up. Your lifestyle can cause this, e.g. if you smoke, don't exercise, and eat an unhealthy diet. Other conditions such as high blood pressure, high cholesterol, or diabetes may also be an issue.

Atheromas can occur in any artery, but they're most common in the ones in your neck which lead to the brain. As well as narrowing the artery, these fatty deposits can break down or become inflamed. This causes a blood clot, which can block the artery or break off and travel through the bloodstream to block an artery in the brain (stroke), or the heart (heart attack).

As with the other conditions in this chapter, lifestyle changes are the most effective way of bringing down your risk of atherosclerosis. However, you may be prescribed medications depending on your personal circumstances. You may be given drugs to manage your cholesterol or blood pressure. In severe cases, you may require surgery.

SIMPLE WAYS TO PREVENT OR SLOW CARDIOVASCULAR DISEASES

As you would have noticed, the best thing you can do to avoid these serious conditions is to make some simple lifestyle changes. The biggest tragedy about the high rate of death from heart attack is that so many of these deaths may have been preventable.

The great thing about making these changes is that they impact on all aspects of your health. You'll be healthier all round, lowering your chances of needing medical support for common problems.

> **Quit smoking.** We all know that smoking has a serious impact on the cardiovascular system. While vaping might seem like a healthier solution, it isn't without risk. Research is still in the early stages. If you struggle to stop by yourself, help is available. Look into local programs, or consider consulting a therapist like a hypnotherapist.
>
> **Dietary Approaches to Stop Hypertension (DASH).** A DASH diet encourages the consumption of foods rich in potassium, calcium, and magnesium. These are all known

to help control blood pressure. It also restricts food high in sodium, saturated fat, and added sugar. Research has shown that DASH could bring down your blood pressure in as little as two weeks[38]. It can also lower your cholesterol levels. You do not need to buy any special foods - you can get everything you need from your local grocery store. Look for lots of vegetables, fruits and whole grains, as well as fish, poultry, beans, and nuts. Cut back on fried foods, and foods high in sugar or salt.

Get moving. Staying active is an important part of a healthy lifestyle. However, if you're new to exercise, consult your health professional first, especially if you know your heart has been damaged.

Meditate. Meditation has been shown to lower blood pressure[39], among many other health benefits. What's more, it's enjoyable and a good way of taking some time out for yourself. I make a point of meditating every day and I believe I'm much calmer as a result. There's nothing like a good Om! to start the day.

MEDICATIONS TO AVOID

If you've been prescribed medication to treat high blood pressure, be aware that some drugs can negatively react with them. These are best avoided or taken with caution. even if you aren't taking any medication for your high blood pressure, some medicines can increase your blood pressure, sending it to dangerous levels.

Prescription and Over-the-Counter Non-steroidal Anti-inflammatory Drugs (NSAIDs). NSAIDs are often used to relieve pain or bring down inflammation. However, they may make your body retain fluid, which can reduce kidney functionality. This will make your blood pressure go up, placing greater strain on your heart and kidneys. They also increase your risk of heart attack or stroke. Ones to be particularly aware of include Ibuprofen (Advil, Motrin) and Naproxen (Aleve, Naprosym). NSAIDs may also be found in many common over-the-counter medications such as cold remedies. When buying an OTC drug, check the label for NSAIDs or consult your pharmacist if you're unsure. They can recommend an alternative for you.

Cough and cold medications. As well as containing NSAIDs, cough and cold remedies often have decongestants. These may make your blood pressure and heart rate rise or interfere with your blood pressure medication. Pseudoephedrine (Sudafed) is particularly known to increase blood pressure. Speak to your doctor or pharmacist about alternatives.

Migraine headache medications. Some migraine medications relieve the pain by tightening blood vessels in your head. Unfortunately, they also constrict blood vessels elsewhere in the body. This can make your blood pressure rise to potentially dangerous levels. Check with your doctor or pharmacist before taking anything to ease your migraine or headache.

Weight loss drugs. Appetite suppressants can increase blood pressure and put strain on the heart. Losing weight is a good thing when it comes to cardiovascular health. Taking medication to speed this process may cause more harm than good, especially since their efficacy is questionable[40].

As with so many health issues, the best treatment is to not get sick in the first place. If you don't want to become one of the 1 in 4 people who die from heart disease, it's time to start living a healthier lifestyle. You don't need me to tell you what to do - we all know smoking and excess drinking are bad for us, while fruit and vegetables are good, but we often don't make healthy choices.

But if you could choose between a life of surgery and pills or one in which you enjoy delicious food and get plenty of exercise, which would you pick? It's a no-brainer, right?

Improving your cardiovascular health improves your overall health. So even if you just start small, you can feel good knowing you're taking steps towards having a long, healthy life.

In the next chapter we're going to look at diabetes, a condition which affects roughly 10% of the population.

DEADLY DIABETES

Three Myths, Two Types Of Diabetes
And One Simple Way To Save A Life

*My body produces insulin like a cow produces rainbows.
It just doesn't happen.*

– Unknown

"You were right."

Those three words always bring mixed emotions. On the one hand, it's great to know that I've helped someone with their health. On the other hand, it often means that someone's discovered that they have a health problem they didn't know about. While it's nice to know they're finally able to get the right treatment, nobody likes to hear that they've got a health issue.

The woman standing in front of me was in her late twenties, professionally dressed. To look at her, you wouldn't think there was anything wrong.

"The steroids they gave me for my eczema pushed up my blood glucose levels. I've got type 2 diabetes! They've given me a prescription for Precose. I'm concerned because they said it might cause weight gain and I really don't want to put on any weight."

"Did your doctor talk to you about diet?" I asked. "Not for weight loss." I hurriedly added, "but to help with your diabetes."

"They gave me a few leaflets, but I haven't read them yet," she told me.

"Well, the main thing is that you eat healthy foods," I said. "Cut back on the amount of sugar you eat, lower your salt intake, and try to eat more fruit and vegetables. The good thing is that eating to help your diabetes will also help with weight control, so hopefully you won't have to worry about taking your meds. But if you've got any problems, any at all, go straight back to your doctor and ask about alternatives."

Diabetes is a complex disease. It isn't a single disorder, but rather a collection of metabolic disorders. They work together, impairing your metabolism of glucose, fats, and proteins.

THREE MISCONCEPTIONS ABOUT DIABETES

1. **Diabetes means you have high blood sugar levels.** In fact, diabetes really means that your blood sugar is uncontrolled. It usually manifests as high blood sugar because people tend to eat a lot of carbs. However, you can have low blood sugar with diabetes.

2. **You should avoid sugar if you have diabetes.** The truth is you need to regulate your sugar intake, not avoid it all together.

3. **If you eat too much sugar you'll get diabetes.** Diabetes is mainly influenced by genetics, although consuming too much sugar can increase your risk. It can also develop during pregnancy, which is known as gestational diabetes. Gestational diabetes usually goes away after giving birth. Women who suffer it are more likely to experience it in subsequent pregnancies and are at greater risk of developing type 2 diabetes.

THE TWO MAIN TYPES OF DIABETES

Type 1 diabetes is caused by an autoimmune disorder of the pancreas. It can only be treated by daily insulin injections.

Type 2 diabetes is caused by impaired insulin production and/or insulin resistance. There are a range of drugs available to help treat this form of diabetes. These include metformin, which helps your cells respond better to insulin and reduces the amount of glucose your intestine absorbs. Lifestyle changes can also help reverse the impact of diabetes.

HOW TO SAVE A LIFE

People with diabetes can suffer life threatening consequences if their blood sugar and insulin levels are imbalanced. Fortunately, it is usually possible to correct these problems if they're identified early enough. Knowing how to identify the early warning signs of a diabetic emergency could save a life.

Hypoglycemia or insulin shock. This is when someone has low blood sugar. It occurs when they have too much insulin in their blood when compared to glucose. This is more common with people with type 1 diabetes but those with type 2 diabetes can also experience it. It can happen if they skip a meal, do more physical activity than usual, drink alcohol, or take too much insulin.

The early warning signs of hypoglycemia include shakiness and hunger. If left untreated it can result in a seizure or even a diabetic coma. It is possible to develop severe hypoglycemia without warning, which is more common in people who've had the condition for a long time. If someone has severe hypoglycemia, they may become confused, suffer blurred vision, have a seizure, or pass out.

If someone indicates that their blood sugar is low, it's important to measure it. If it is the case, the best method to help them balance their blood sugar is by following the 15/15 rule: eat 15 grams of fast acting carbs, e.g. glucose tablets, fruit juice, soda, honey, or sugar, and wait 15 minutes. If they don't feel better, repeat and test the blood sugar again.

If someone has passed out due to hypoglycemia, this is a medical emergency. If possible, give them a glucagon shot and call for emergency help. They should wake up within 15 minutes of getting the glucagon. Encourage them to sip regular soda or fruit juice while you're waiting for help.

Diabetic ketoacidosis (DKA). This is a life-threatening emergency caused when the body doesn't have enough insulin. This makes your liver break down fat into ketones for energy, but too fast for the body to process. The ketones build up in the blood, which could make you fall into a coma. DKA is most common with type 1 diabetes but can also occur with type 2 and gestational diabetes. It may be a result of not having injected enough insulin, not eating enough, or blood sugar levels dropping during sleep. It can also occur if you're sick or get an infection. Some medications or a big stress such as a heart attack can also cause it.

The early symptoms of DKA are extreme thirst, a dry mouth and needing to urinate more frequently. More serious symptoms include fatigue, dry or flushed skin, a fruity smell to the breath, nausea, vomiting, or stomach ache, problems breathing, feeling woozy, confused, or passing out.

If someone has the early symptoms, get them to test their urine with a ketone test kit. If their ketone levels are high, call a doctor. If they have serious signs, go straight to the emergency room.

Hyperosmolar Hyperglycemic Syndrome (HHS). High blood sugar or hyperglycemia isn't as common as DKA but is more dangerous. It's a complication of type 2 diabetes caused by having high blood sugar with little or no ketones. HHS is most common in older people with uncontrolled diabetes who are sick or have an infection. Their blood sugar rises over time, so the body tries to eliminate the excess glucose by urinating more frequently. If they don't drink enough to compensate they get dehydrated and develop HHS. Left untreated, HHS can cause seizures, coma, and death.

Symptoms include a dry mouth, cool hands and feet, skin warm to the touch but no sweating, high heart rate, high fever (over 101F), constant thirst, frequent urination, dark urine, nausea, vomiting, stomach ache, confusion, hallucinations, slurred speech, and weakness down one side of the body.

If you suspect someone is suffering from HHS call their doctor and get them to the emergency room as soon as possible.

Preeclampsia. If you have any type of diabetes when you're pregnant, either type 1, type 2, or gestational, you are at a higher risk of developing preeclampsia. This can send your blood pressure sky high, putting both your and your baby's health at risk. It may be that the baby has to be immediately delivered, even if they're not full term. It is also possible to develop preeclampsia after delivery, even if you didn't have it when you were pregnant.

Women with preeclampsia often don't feel sick or think their symptoms are normal. Some of the more serious symptoms include blurred vision, seeing spots/flashing lights, a sensitivity to light, persistent headache, severe swelling of the face, hands, and feet, pain under the right ribs or in the right shoulder, low back pain, sudden weight gain, vomiting late in pregnancy, anxiety, and sudden shortness of breath.

If you suspect preeclampsia, call the doctor immediately. Medical care may be immediately required.

IMPORTANT INFORMATION ABOUT DIABETES

Around 1 in 10 Americans have diabetes - that's 37.3 million. Approximately 1 in 5 people with diabetes don't know they have it. In addition, 96 million American adults - that's over 1 in 3 - have prediabetes. Over 8 in 10 adults with prediabetes don't know they have it[41]. The earlier diabetes can be identified the better. Early intervention can stop more serious problems developing.

Anyone can develop diabetes, regardless of age, sex, or ethnicity. If a blood relative develops diabetes, you are at increased risk, so it's especially important to be aware of any changes in your health should you have these genetic traits.

No two people's symptoms are the same, but the most common are:

- Needing to go to the toilet a lot, especially during night-time
- Feeling thirsty all the time
- Increased levels of tiredness
- Unexplained weight loss
- Genital itching or thrush
- Slow-healing cuts and wounds
- Blurry eyesight
- Increased hunger.

One way of identifying diabetes in children can be to check the 4Ts - toilet, thirsty, thinner, and tiredness.

TESTING YOUR BLOOD SUGAR LEVELS AT HOME

If you have diabetes, self-testing your blood sugar levels is an important part of controlling your condition and avoiding complications. You may be given a device known as a continuous glucose monitor (CGM). Alternatively you can quickly test your blood sugar at home using a blood sugar meter and a small drop of your blood.

Regular testing helps you:

- Monitor the effect of your diabetes medications

- Know when your blood sugar levels are high or low
- Track your progress towards your treatment goals
- Learn how diet and exercise impacts your blood sugar levels
- Identify the impact of other factors like stress or illness on your blood sugar.

Your healthcare provider will tell you how often to check your blood sugar levels. It will vary depending on what type of diabetes you have and your treatment plan. If you have type 1 diabetes you may need to test up to 10 times a day. If you have type 2 diabetes, you'll usually need to test before meals and bedtime if you're taking daily injections of insulin. If you're managing your condition with diet and exercise or non-insulin medications, you may not need to test as frequently.

You'll need a blood sugar meter to test your blood. Even if you have a continuous glucose monitor (CGM), you'll still need to test your blood to ensure your CGM is properly calibrated.

Speak to your health care provider or diabetes specialist about which device is right for you. They can also talk you through using your meter. As a general guide:

- Wash and dry your hands because food or dirt can negate the reading.
- Insert a test strip into the meter.

- Prick the side of your fingertip with the lancet provided. (While you can also take blood from your forearm or palm, the results will be less accurate.)

- Touch and hold the edge of the test strip to the drop of blood.

- After a few seconds, you'll see your blood sugar level displayed on the screen.

MONITORING THE PROGRESS OF YOUR TREATMENT

Your doctor should explain to you your ideal blood sugar target range. It's important to try and maintain your blood sugar levels within this range to avoid developing more serious health problems. Keeping your blood sugar levels consistent can also help your energy levels and mood.

Typical targets are to have a blood sugar level of 80-130 mg/dL before a meal and less than 180 mg/dL two hours after eating. A blood sugar below 70 mg/dL is considered low. There may be a slight variation to these numbers depending on your age, overall health and other factors. Discuss with your health care team about the right targets for you.

TESTING YOUR HBA1C

Your HbA1c is your average blood glucose level for the previous 2-3 months. If you have diabetes, you should aim for an HbA1c level of 48mmol/mol (6.5%) or lower. If you're at risk of developing type 2 diabetes, you should try to have a target HbA1c level of below

42mmol/mol (6%). HbA1c is what's known as glycated hemoglobin which is made when the glucose in your body sticks to the red blood cells. Your body can't use this sugar properly, so it builds up in the blood. Your HbA1c is usually tested quarterly because red blood cells are active for 2-3 months, although it might be tested more or less frequently than this depending on your personal circumstances.

The results of your HbA1c test will let your healthcare team know if your treatment or medication requires adjustment. They will be able to tell you your target range. You might find it helpful to write your results in your Workbook to identify any trends. Your HbA1c can change for a range of reasons, including illness, the impact of other medicines, lifestyle changes, stress, or depression.

HOW TO DEAL WITH DIABETES

Diabetes doesn't have to mean you give up the things you love. There are a number of things you can do to ensure you live as normal a life as possible.

LIFESTYLE CHANGES

Some people find that they can control their diabetes through making some lifestyle changes. In fact, some with type 2 diabetes find symptoms go away completely if they overhaul their diet and avoid smoking and drinking.

Recommended lifestyle changes may include:

- Doing 2½ hours of moderate physical activity every week or 1¼ hours of high intensity exercise.
- Losing weight to have a healthy body mass index. (More on this in the next chapter.)
- Replacing refined carbohydrates with wholegrain foods. Eating more vegetables and foods high in dietary fiber.
- Lowering the amount of saturated fat in your diet.
- Stopping smoking and drinking alcohol.

Everyone's situation is different, so speak to your healthcare team before making any major changes.

MEDICATIONS

It may be that your diabetes requires treatment with medication. There are a number of different options available which work in different ways. Not all treatments are right for everyone, so you may need to switch medications or try different combinations to find the best one for you.

Some of the most common medications include:

Metformin. This is usually the first diabetes medication to be prescribed for type 2 diabetes if lifestyle changes aren't enough.

Sulphonylureas. This is a family of tablets which stimulate the cells in the pancreas to make more insulin and help insulin to be more effective.

Acarbose. This is from a family of medication called alpha-glucosidase inhibitors. It slows down the absorption of starchy food, slowing down the increase in blood sugar levels.

Repaglinide and Nateglinide. These are prandial glucose regulators and should be taken half an hour before meals, up to three times a day. They are similar to sulphonylureas but have a faster but shorter effect on insulin production. They shouldn't be taken if you miss a meal because this could cause low blood sugar levels.

Pioglitazone. These help your body use its natural insulin more effectively. It also protects the cells in the pancreas so you can produce insulin for longer.

Incretin mimetics. These injections increase the production of incretins, hormones which help the production of insulin. In addition, they lower the amount of sugar produced by the liver, slowing down digestion and depressing the appetite.

Statins. These help lower levels of bad cholesterol. Diabetes increases your risk of heart diseases, so it's important to keep your cholesterol levels down.

Every person with diabetes is different. Keep an open dialog with your healthcare team to make sure you've got the right treatment plan. Diabetes medications are safe, but they may have side effects or interact with other medications. Discuss the possibility of these with your healthcare team. Remember you can always talk to your friendly neighborhood pharmacist for more details about what to watch out for.

FOR EXCELLENT HEALTH DO THIS

You may find some of your medications come with extra benefits, like helping you lose weight or protecting your heart or kidneys. If you have any doubt or confusion, talk to your healthcare team about why they're giving you a particular medication.

Read the patient information leaflet with your medication for details about what side effects to expect. The most common include:

- Weight loss
- Weight gain
- Bloating
- Diarrhea
- Nausea

If you suffer a severe side effect or reaction, remember to seek medical assistance immediately. Be aware that many other medications interfere with diabetes drugs. For example, some asthma meds can mask the symptoms of hypoglycemia, so you don't know you should seek treatment. If you are on any medications, tell your medical team before they prescribe you something for your diabetes. Likewise, if you need any drugs for a different condition, make sure you give the prescribing medic a full list of everything you're currently taking.

Use your Workbook to log your diabetes symptoms and experiences. This will make it easier for your healthcare team to make any necessary adjustments to your treatment plan. This supports you to continue to enjoy a good quality of life.

USEFUL SUPPLEMENTS FOR PEOPLE WITH DIABETES

Keeping glucose tablets to hand is always a good idea in case of a drop in blood sugar levels. There are some other supplements which may be a good idea to help your condition. As always, discuss with your healthcare team before starting to take any supplements.

> **Manganese.** Manganese deficiency is common among diabetics and there is a (as yet unproven) theory it could be part of the cause of diabetes.
>
> **Magnesium.** Magnesium levels drop in people with diabetes. It may become dangerously low if you have severe diabetic retinopathy. Magnesium deficiency has also been shown to have a direct impact on the blood sugar control of type 2 diabetics[42]. If you are taking supplemental magnesium, you may find you can lower your insulin dosage.
>
> **Potassium.** Taking insulin may result in a deficiency of potassium. If you take potassium supplements you may improve your sensitivity to insulin and its effectiveness.
>
> **Taurine.** Type 1 diabetics often have low levels of taurine which can impact on the thickness of blood, increasing the risk of heart disease. Taking taurine supplements may help improve levels of blood viscosity[43].
>
> **Vitamin C.** Type 1 diabetics often have low levels of vitamin C. Increasing the amount of vitamin C in the bloodstream may lower the amount of sorbitol. This is a harmful sugar

which may raise the risk of diabetic complications. Type 2 diabetics may find tat vitamin C improves their glucose tolerance[44].

Zinc. Zinc deficiency has been proposed as a possible cause of diabetes. It may be crucial for the effective metabolism of insulin. It also protects against viral infections and may protect beta cells from destruction. Type 1 diabetics often have a zinc deficiency and in some cases, taking zinc supplements has lowered blood sugar levels[45].

Diabetes doesn't have to be a life limiting condition. Self-awareness is key. If you regularly monitor your blood sugar levels and practice healthy habits, there's no reason you can't have the same quality of life as anyone else.

One of the risk factors in developing type 2 diabetes is being obese. So in the next chapter, we're going to look more at how to know what your healthy weight is and how to achieve and maintain it.

8

MANAGING YOUR WEIGHT

4 Reasons To Get In Shape And The Right Way To Do It

You didn't gain all your weight in one day;
you won't lose it in one day. Be patient with yourself.

– Jenna Wolfe

FOR EXCELLENT HEALTH DO THIS

"Do I look fat to you?"

It's a question no man ever wants to be asked! Fortunately for me, it seemed to be rhetorical, as the woman in front of me carried on talking.

"My boyfriend says I need to lose weight, but I think I look great."

"Well, you know what they say," I joked. "If you want to lose a couple hundred pounds, get rid of the boyfriend!"

She laughed with me. "Maybe I might just do that. It's not like we've been seeing each other for long. Still, last time I weighed myself I was 180lb. Maybe he has a point. Don't they say that if you're over 170kg you're obese?"

"They might say that, but that doesn't mean they're right," I told her. "There are a lot of factors which go into whether someone's obese or not. It's not just about numbers on a scale or BMI."

"BMI?" Her forehead wrinkled in a frown.

"Body Mass Index," I explained. "It's calculated by dividing your weight by the square of your height. If you've got a BMI of over 25 then you're overweight. A BMI over 30 means you're obese and if it's over 40 then you're morbidly obese. You're pretty tall for a woman, so it may be that your BMI is around 25."

"So maybe I'm not fat!"

"Exactly." I smiled at how happy she looked. "But BMI doesn't tell the whole story because it doesn't take into account muscle mass. For example, a lot of bodybuilders have a very high BMI, but they have hardly any fat - it's all muscle. You'll hear people say that muscle weighs more than fat and technically that's not true. A pound of fat will weigh the same as a pound of muscle."

The woman snapped her fingers. "They both weigh a pound!"

"Right. But muscle's denser, so it takes up less space. If you really want to know whether you're overweight or not, you're better off not focusing on the numbers on the scale and looking more at the measurements around your hips and waist, as well as how your body looks. Ultimately, your weight is only one factor in being healthy - yes, it's an important one, but just because you're slim doesn't mean you're fit and just because you've got a higher BMI doesn't mean you can't be healthy. If I were you, I'd look at your overall health and then decide whether you want to lose a few pounds. Don't let a boyfriend dictate how you take care of yourself."

"Don't worry. I won't."

You hear a lot about the so-called obesity epidemic and it's true that more people are overweight now than in the past. There's one basic explanation for this: the difference between calorie intake and calories used. But there's a more complex picture at play to explain why one person can stuff their face with pizza and cake and not seem to put on any weight while someone else only has to look at a chocolate bar and they'll pile on the pounds.

Some of the factors which can contribute to weight gain include:

- Medications, such as the ones to treat diabetes or epilepsy.

- Medical conditions like hypothyroidism, or depression.
- Environmental factors like eating habits or a sedentary lifestyle.
- Genetics. However, it's worth noting that while often parents with a weight problem have children with a weight problem, this may also be due to diet and exercise habits rather than genetics.

FOUR REASONS TO GET IN SHAPE

Lowers the chances of developing other health problems. You'll have noticed that diet and exercise have featured when I've discussed ways of treating or even avoiding health conditions. I'm all in favor of body positivity and I think the most important thing is for anyone to feel comfortable in their skin. But it cannot be avoided that obesity has been directly linked to an increased risk of serious conditions like stroke[46], heart problems[47], diabetes[48], polycystic ovary syndrome[49], and cancer[50]. It's also been linked to a number of other less serious conditions, such as gout. One of the best things you can do for yourself is to maintain a healthy weight.

Reduces the risk of problems with medications. Many medications have to be adjusted to your weight. Obese people may find it harder to get the right dose to treat their condition.

Improves the quality of your life. While many obese people still manage to live an active life, others find it difficult. Losing weight can give your energy levels a boost, making you feel more positive. As little as 5% weight loss can have a major impact on your blood pressure, glucose tolerance, and cholesterol levels. This can in turn reduce your risk of developing the conditions mentioned earlier.

Boosts your confidence. Beauty goes much deeper than how you look. Everyone is beautiful regardless of size, so your self-esteem shouldn't be connected to your weight. However, the sad truth is that losing weight may improve your self-esteem if you feel uncomfortable with your body.

LOSING WEIGHT EFFECTIVELY

This is a huge subject. It will take much more than a chapter in a book to delve into effective weight loss. However, I'm going to give you a little overview of what you can do to lose weight and keep it off.

Unfortunately, there isn't a quick and easy way to lose weight. You will have to make changes to your diet and increase the amount of exercise you get. Resistance training and aerobics are important so you don't lose muscle mass along with fat, as well as improve your cardio function. However, for some people, a strict diet and exercise regime still doesn't seem to give them the results they want. In these cases medication may be appropriate or even bariatric surgery.

DIETING: THE GOOD, THE BAD, AND THE UGLY

I really don't like the concept of diets. Realistically, you should be viewing your approach to food as a lifestyle change rather than a diet. Frequently what happens with a diet is that people lose weight while they're sticking to it. The second they stop dieting the weight piles back on, usually with an extra pound or two for good measure!

For example, the keto diet is very popular right now. It was developed to mimic fasting without actually starving yourself as a way of treating epilepsy. It's a low carb, high fat diet similar to the Atkins diet which is aimed at bringing on a state of ketosis which usually only occurs during fasting. As such, it can induce rapid weight loss without needing to stop eating. In the long term, it may cause low blood pressure, kidney stones, constipation, nutrient deficiencies and an elevated risk of heart disease[51].

Another popular diet is the paleo or paleolithic diet, which includes lean meats, fish, fruits, vegetables, nuts and seeds. These are foods which could be easily obtained by hunting and gathering. The aim is to get back to what might be considered a more natural diet for humans. As such, more recent additions to our diet, such as dairy products, legumes, and grains, are to be avoided.

The problem with the paleo diet is this lack of whole grains and legumes, natural sources of fiber, vitamins and nutrients. Cutting out dairy products also means you may struggle to get enough protein and calcium. Another issue is the simple fact that these 'forbidden' foods aren't just healthy, they're also more affordable than the staples of the paleo diet. Some people might find that a paleo diet is out of their budget.

You might have heard people talk about the Mediterranean diet. This is less of a diet and more of a food philosophy inspired by the eating habits of people from the Mediterranean region. It encourages a high consumption of fruit, vegetables, unrefined grains, olive oil, legumes, and fish, a moderate consumption of dairy and lean meat and a minimal consumption of red meat and sweets. Unlike other diets, it doesn't explicitly exclude anything. Research into whether it can help protect against conditions like heart disease or high blood pressure is being carried out. However, it can be difficult to know what you should eat because it's such a loose set of principles and nothing is off the table, so to speak. If you try to follow a predominantly plant-based diet, you can't go far wrong. Following a Mediterranean diet is a good way of starting a healthier way of eating.

Intermittent fasting is a different approach to dieting because it focuses on **when** you eat rather than **what** you eat. Like Paleo, intermittent fasting draws its inspiration from the past. Even just 50 years ago it was easier to maintain a healthy weight because there weren't multiple devices in every home. TV shows stopped broadcasting at 11pm, so people stopped eating because they'd gone to bed. Portions were smaller and the range of food was limited. Now the internet means we stay up later to watch TV, play games and chat online, often snacking while we do.

Intermittent fasting involves establishing a regular pattern of eating and fasting. The theory is that after hours without food, the body has worked through its sugar stores and instead starts burning fat. You could try eating during an 8-hour period every day and then fast for the rest of the time. You might want to limit yourself to just one 500-600 calorie meal two days a week. There's no strict guidance to what you should be eating when you're not fasting. Still, it's a good idea to choose healthy foods rather than stuffing yourself with cake and sweets. The Mediterranean diet can be a good combination with fasting.

You should **always** consult your doctor before starting intermittent fasting. They can advise you on a safe way to practice it. Going too long without eating might encourage your body to store fat as a reaction to starvation. They can also give you guidance on what to eat.

Adjusting what you eat as part of a weight loss program involves switching out high-calorie meals with low-calorie alternatives. While it might take a while to get used to new types of food, you may find they are just as delicious if not more so.

WEIGHT LOSS MEDICATIONS

There are a lot of medications advertised which promise miraculous weight loss. Any quick fix pill should be handled with caution. It's highly unlikely they can do what they claim and they can be extremely dangerous. People have died from weight loss medications[52].

If you feel you need the support of weight loss medications, consult your doctor so you can use them responsibly.

> **Orlistat** is the only OTC medication with FDA approval for weight loss in conjunction with a reduced calorie diet. It works by inhibiting the absorption of dietary fats by around 30%. There are few side effects associated with it, which are mainly associated with gastrointestinal problems such as flatulence, fatty or oily stools, and

abdominal pain or discomfort. A rare side effect is severe liver injury. If you start to display any symptoms of liver injury, such as yellowish eyes or skin, dark urine, or fever, stop taking the medication and consult your healthcare provider immediately. Patients taking Orlistat may find it harder to absorb fat-soluble vitamins A, D, E and K. It's recommended you take a multivitamin containing these vitamins to maintain your levels. Take the multivitamin at least two hours before or after taking orlistat.

Phentermine is taken as part of a program including diet and exercise for a maximum of a few weeks. After that it stops having an effect. Since it can increase the risk of stroke, it is important to monitor your blood pressure while taking it. Don't renew the course once you've finished your pills. It is also available in combination with topiramate. It is not advised if you are pregnant or breastfeeding or if you're taking SSRIs or MAO inhibitors. It works to suppress the appetite. Common side effects include faster heart beat, high blood pressure, insomnia, restlessness and dizziness. It was withdrawn in the UK in 2000 due to potential heart damage, although it is still available in the US.

Fluoxetine is an antidepressant which may cause weight loss when taken in conjunction with a diet and exercise regime. One of its side effects is to repress the appetite so it may help weight loss in sufferers of depression. However, it's not a long term solution. As your depression symptoms alleviate, your appetite is likely to return. Moreover, if you don't have depression, there is no evidence to show antidepressants help more than diet and exercise on their own.

WEIGHT LOSS SUPPLEMENTS

It's tempting to turn to supplements or herbal remedies to help you lose weight. It's easy to think that if it's natural, it's a healthy way to support your weight loss journey. However, research is mixed or even non-existent and some supplements come with health risks. The FDA doesn't regulate supplements in the same way as other medications, so they're not reviewed for safety or efficacy before coming to market. In addition, the FDA has come down hard on some weight loss supplements containing prescription drugs not listed on the label. If you decide you'd like to take supplements to help with your weight, consult your doctor first.

Some of the most popular weight loss supplements include:

Chitosan. This is a sugar made from the hard outer layers of lobsters, crabs, and shrimp. It is claimed it stops fats and cholesterol from being absorbed by your body. Natural Medicines, an independent group which analyzes research into supplements, says there isn't enough evidence to support this claim. The National Center for Complementary and Integrative Health says that it has not been proven to be effective. It rarely causes side effects, although some people find they get an upset stomach or constipation. t should be avoided if you're allergic to shellfish.

Green Tea Extract. This is alleged to limit your appetite as well as burn more calories and fat. Natural Medicines says there is scant evidence for its efficacy. Side effects include nausea, vomiting, bloating, gas, diarrhea, dizziness, and insomnia.

Green Coffee Extract. There are some studies which suggest it can result in modest weight loss. However, Natural Medicines holds that there isn't enough robust evidence to prove its effectiveness. Side effects are rare, but because it contains caffeine, green coffee extract may cause headaches, stomach upset, anxiety, insomnia, and abnormal heart rhythms.

Guar Gum. This is extracted from the seed of the guar plant. It's supposed to prevent fats from being absorbed into your body and help you feel fuller faster. It has been studied more than other natural weight loss products. The general consensus is that it's ineffective. It may cause gas or diarrhea.

Ephedra. This herb is also known as ma huang and naturally contains ephedrine, a stimulant. The FDA banned supplements containing ephedra after it was found to cause serious side effects including heart attack, arrhythmia, stroke, psychosis, seizures, and death. The FDA states that there is little evidence that the herb helps beyond short-term weight loss. Any benefits are outweighed by the risks.

Bitter Orange. The rind of bitter oranges contains synephrine, a stimulant related to ephedrine. It allegedly increases the amount of calories burned. After the FDA banned weight loss products containing ephedra, many manufacturers started using bitter orange. It's unclear if this is a safer option. Natural Medicines say it is possibly unsafe when taken orally as a supplement and there isn't enough evidence to show whether it promotes weight loss. Some studies found that it can raise your blood pressure and heart rate. Some people have experienced dangerous side effects either from taking it alone or when combined with other stimulants like caffeine. These include stroke, irregular heartbeat, heart attack, and death. The FDA has stated that bitter orange may not be safe as a dietary supplement. It should definitely be avoided if you have a heart condition, high blood pressure, or if you take caffeine, medications like MAO inhibitors, or any herbs or supplements which affect the heart rate.

BARIATRIC SURGERIES

Bariatric surgeries can be the best option for morbidly obese people who have a BMI of over 40 or people with a BMI of over 35 who also suffer from comorbid conditions like hypertension, heart disease, diabetes, etc.

There are a number of different types of bariatric surgeries, so you should speak to an appropriate healthcare professional about which one is right for you.

> **A gastric bypass** is where surgical staples create a small pouch at the top of the stomach before it's attached to the small intestine to bypass the rest of the stomach. It takes less food to make you feel full and you'll absorb fewer calories when you do eat.
>
> **A gastric band** is a band placed around the stomach to create a small pouch near the top. It takes less food to fill the pouch, so less food is required to fill you up. The band can be tightened after surgery until you find the right tightness for you.

A sleeve gastrectomy involves removing most of the stomach so you need less food to satiate your appetite.

An intra-gastric balloon is an air or salt-water filled soft balloon placed in your stomach via a thin tube passed down your throat. You won't be able to eat as much before feeling full, but it is only a temporary solution, lasting a maximum of 6 months.

A biliopancreatic diversion is like a gastric bypass, only the stomach pouch is connected further along the small intestine. This results in even fewer calories being absorbed but because it has more side effects than a gastric bypass it's less frequently performed.

Primary obesity surgery endolumenal is a cutting edge technique to shrink the stomach. A tube called an endoscope is passed into your stomach, and then the surgeon uses this to gain access for tiny tools to gather the stomach into folds, making it smaller.

You should bear in mind that approximately 50% of patients regain weight within 24 months of having surgery[53]. In addition, bariatric surgery is exactly that - a type of surgery which threfore comes with inherent risks.

Some of the more common immediate side effects include:

- Acid reflux
- Complications from anesthesia
- Nausea and vomiting

- An inability to eat certain foods
- Infection
- Stomach obstruction
- Weight gain

Long-term side effects can range from mild to severe, including:

- Dumping syndrome (Food from the stomach goes straight to the large intestine without being properly digested)
- Low blood sugar
- Malnutrition
- Vomiting
- Ulcers
- Bowel obstruction
- Hernias

TALKING TO YOUR HEALTHCARE PROVIDERS ABOUT YOUR WEIGHT

It is a sad reality that many people suffering from weight issues don't always have positive interactions with healthcare professionals. Doctors may dismiss symptoms as being simply down to weight instead of something else.

However, there's also a lot of help available. Nutritionists and dieticians can help you put together an appropriate plan to help you adjust your diet. Psychotherapists can support you to deal with any underlying issues which may be preventing you from losing weight. And, of course, your friendly neighborhood pharmacist is always happy to help give you advice on how to start losing weight!

The more you can be open with your healthcare team about your relationship with your weight and your personal goals, the more likely you'll be able to set realistic targets and meet them.

Having faced my own issues with weight at various times in my life, I know all too well how it can impact your overall health. That's why in the next chapter, we're going to look at something we all experience at one time or another - pain.

You'll find a very simple and useful form in your Workbook to get you on the right track towards weight management by just measuring the basics - how you eat and whether you move. Get that started now. It will pay enormous dividends www.learnwellbooks.com/healthy

PAIN

10 Simple Ways To Manage It

Pain is inevitable, suffering is optional.
– *Buddhist proverb*

One of the most common reasons for people to come to me is to get help with pain. Pain affects all of us and can strike at any time. There are many different types of pain, but they all carry fairly common messages: to warn you about tissue damage and problems so you can minimize injury, get some rest, or seek medical assistance. I've had many, many conversations with people about how they can manage their pain.

There was one man, Nick, who'd been regularly coming into my pharmacy to pick up various different types of pain relief. He'd told me how he'd tried everything - pills, creams, supplements, but his pain had been getting worse and worse. It had started as a minor irritation, but as time wore on, it hurt for him to walk, sit, lie down, do anything. He'd started using a cane to get around and I'd hated seeing someone fit and healthy decline so quickly.

But this time was different. Nick was still using his cane, but as he approached the counter, there was a big smile on his face.

"I've had some good news, James," he told me. "They've finally found what's wrong with me. I've got hypermobile Ehlers-Danlos Syndrome."

Hypermobile Ehlers-Danlos syndrome is a genetic connective tissue disorder which causes hypermobile joints, fragile skin, and autonomic dysfunction, a form of nerve damage.

"It must be such a relief for you to have answers," I said.

"I know, right?" Nick's smile broadened. "All those doctors who made me feel like I was going crazy when there was an explanation all along."

"So how did you get your diagnosis?"

"It was more luck than anything else," Nick told me. "I got talking to a nurse while I was waiting for an appointment and she mentioned that her aunt had EDS. I asked my doctor about it and she agreed it sounded possible, so she ordered some tests and I finally had an explanation for how I've been feeling."

"Sometimes all it takes is that one person who's had the same experience, doesn't it?" I was so pleased for him. "So what can I do for you today? Do you need some more pain relief?"

"Actually, I just want some Band Aids and antihistamines," Nick said. "I've found that there are better ways of coping with my pain than constantly popping pills. And it's not like it's all that healthy to keep taking painkillers. Nowadays I listen to my body and rest if that's what I need. I make sure I eat regularly and keep myself well hydrated. I've discovered myofascial release techniques, so I give myself a massage on the right trigger points which really helps. I've even started meditating." Nick laughed. "I'm the last person I ever thought would do that, but I've found that I enjoy it."

"That's great news. I'm so glad you've found something which works for you."

"Don't get me wrong," Nick said. "I still have my bad days. But I've found other ways of coping. I have a Tumblr filled with funny memes or I binge watch Netflix to take my mind off things. There were days when I felt like I didn't want to go on because I was in so much pain, but now I've figured out how to deal with it and life's so much better."

For many people, pain is a fact of daily life. For others, it's an occasional experience with a clearly defined cause. It's possible to experience more than one type of pain at the same time. However you feel, if you can pinpoint the type of pain you're suffering it'll help your healthcare professional identify the possible cause and put together an effective treatment plan. Pharmacists such as myself have a wealth of information about pain relief and we're always happy to discuss your options.

ACUTE PAIN

Acute pain occurs over a short period and usually comes on suddenly. Possible causes include:

> **Injury** e.g. cuts, burns, muscle strains, bone fractures, etc.
>
> **Illness** e.g. food poisoning, appendicitis, meningitis, etc.
>
> **Medical procedures** e.g. dental work, surgery, injections, etc.

Acute pain tends to be sharp and generally goes away within a short period of time after the cause has been dealt with.

CHRONIC PAIN

Chronic pain lasts for a prolonged period of time. It can vary in intensity, coming and going so the sufferer has good and bad days. Many health conditions cause chronic pain, such as arthritis, fibromyalgia, cancer, or Ehlers-Danlos Syndrome. Some injuries can also cause chronic pain even after the original injury has healed.

Chronic pain affects approximately 20% of people and is one of the main reasons why people seek medical assistance[54].

FUNCTIONAL PAIN

In some instances, such as in Nick's case, it can be difficult to determine the cause of chronic pain. Even after extensive testing, some people suffer chronic pain without any evidence of injury or illness. This is called functional pain and it's usually chronic, although it is possible to experience acute functional pain.

NOCICEPTIVE PAIN

Nociceptive pain is caused by tissue damage. This might be due to injury but it can also come from certain health conditions which cause tissue inflammation and damage, such as osteoporosis, arthritis, inflammatory bowel disease (IBD).

Nociceptive pain can be acute or chronic depending on the cause and can feel achy, throbbing, or sharp. If you develop nociceptive pain in your skin, muscles, ligaments, tendons, joints, or bones, it's called somatic pain. If you're suffering it in your internal organs, this is visceral pain.

NEUROPATHIC PAIN

Neuropathic pain is the result of nerve damage. You may suffer neuropathic pain if a disc in your spine slips or if you develop certain conditions like shingles, diabetes, cancer, or multiple sclerosis.

Neuropathic pain is usually chronic, although it is possible to experience acute neuropathic pain. It can manifest as a stabbing, shooting, burning, or prickling sensation. In addition, you may feel hypersensitive to touch, movement or extremes in temperature.

TEN WAYS TO MANAGE YOUR PAIN

If you're suffering pain and are unsure of the cause or the best way to manage it, don't be afraid to consult your healthcare team. There is a lot that can be done to relieve pain, so it's a case of finding the best approach for you.

1. **NSAIDS (Non-steroidal anti-inflammatory drugs)** are frequently used to relieve pain, lower inflammation and combat fever. They can be effective against the symptoms of headaches, period pain, sprains and strains, colds and flu, arthritis, etc. However, they're not suitable for everyone and can cause side effects. You should check with your doctor or pharmacist before taking them if:

    a. You're over 65 or under 16
    b. Are pregnant, trying to conceive, or breastfeeding
    c. Suffer from asthma
    d. Have had an allergic reaction to NSAIDs
    e. Have a stomach ulcer
    f. Have problems with your heart, liver, kidneys, blood pressure, or bowels
    g. Are taking any medications.

2. **Sprays and creams** are good for treating localized pain. Deep heat, deep freeze, capsaicin, creams, diclofenac creams can all help relieve muscular aches and pains.

3. **Muscle relaxants** such as Sirdalud are used to treat discomfort due to acute musculoskeletal conditions like stiffness, tension, rigidity, and muscle spasms.

4. **Buscopan** is part of the antimuscarinics family of drugs used to treat cramps like stomach cramps, bladder cramps, and period pain.

5. **PPIs (Proton pump inhibitors)** such as omeprazole and lansoprazole are medicines which reduce the amount of stomach your stomach produces. This relieves the pain caused by ulcers and other types of pain in your chest or stomach, easing any inflammation.

6. **A TENS (Transcutaneous electrical nerve stimulation) machine** delivers small electrical impulses to the affected part of your body. This can reduce the pain signals going to the spinal cord and brain which may reduce pain and relax muscles. Some people swear by them while others find it irritating. They are safe to use, although there is a small risk of burning or irritation if the current is too high or the electrodes are placed on the wrong part of the body.

7. **Acupuncture** stimulates sensory nerves under the skin and in the muscles by inserting very thin needles through the skin at specific points in the body. It is usually painless, although some people do experience discomfort when the needles are first put in place. There is good evidence

for its effectiveness and side effects are minimal when it's practiced by an appropriately qualified professional[55].

8. **Relaxation therapies** such as meditation have been shown to have a positive impact on pain[56]. Meditation doesn't have to be complex - just taking a few moments to focus on your breath and observe its flow in and out of your body can help calm you and distract you from the pain.

9. **Hot and cold compresses** can be used to treat anything from arthritis to pulled muscles. Hot and cold compresses can be a highly effective way of relieving pain at a low cost. As a general rule, use ice if you've suffered an acute injury or pain and there's inflammation or swelling. Avoid cold compresses if you have nerve damage, poor circulation or lessened sensitivity. Don't use on stiff muscles or joints. Use heat to treat muscle pain or stiffness. Be careful not to make the compress too hot or you might cause a burn. Don't use if there is any swelling, bruising, or an open wound. Likewise, if you have a condition such as diabetes, dermatitis, vascular diseases, deep vein thrombosis, or multiple sclerosis, you shouldn't use a hot compress. If you have heart disease, hypertension, or are pregnant, check with your doctor before using any form of heat therapy.

10. **Home remedies** can be an effective way of treating pain. For example, lavender essential oil can be a natural pain reliever. A small-scale 2012 study[57] found that it was better at treating migraines than a placebo. Since the FDA doesn't regulate essential oils, make sure to source your oils from a reputable source and consult your doctor

before using them. A surprising treatment for headache is coffee. Certain chemicals in coffee bind to and block the adenosine receptors to reduce pain. They also stimulate the release of dopamine and beta-endorphins, the body's natural pain killers. Many over-the-counter analgesics have caffeine included because of its pain relieving properties. A standard dose of one of these painkillers taken with a mug of coffee has been shown to reduce the amount of pain experienced by 5-10%[58] as compared to just taking a pill. It is worth bearing in mind that your tolerance to caffeine builds up over time, so if you are a habitual coffee drinker, you'll find you need to drink more to experience the same effect.

If you're suffering any form of pain, it's always best to discuss it with your doctor or pharmacist before self-medicating. While there's a lot you can do to help yourself, not all home remedies are suitable for everyone and if you're using an inappropriate form of pain relief, it can cause more harm than good.

If you're pregnant, you need to be especially careful about what you take to deal with pain, which is why in the next chapter we're going to look at what you can and can't do for your health when you're expecting.

Your Workbook features a useful pain tracker that will help with any discussions you have with your medical team about your pain history. We hope you're not currently experiencing pain but open your Journal to become familiar with the tracker now.

Get your copy at www.learnwellbooks.com/healthy

10

A HAPPY PREGNANCY

... And A Paradox

We have a secret in our culture, and it's not that birth is painful. It's that women are strong.

– Laura Stavoe Harm

A friend of my family suffered from bipolar disorder. I'll call her Marie. She desperately wanted to have a baby, but she'd been told that she shouldn't even think about getting pregnant because she was taking lithium. She was advised that she wouldn't be able to stop taking it because it was too dangerous, but lithium would harm the baby, so she would have to look at alternatives, like surrogacy.

Marie was determined not to give up on her dream of becoming a mum. Eventually, she found a perinatal specialist who was able to talk through all the options and associated risks. She made the decision to slowly wean herself off lithium and move onto other medications, which were safer in pregnancy.

While she was trying to fall pregnant, Marie did have some struggles. She told me she used a mood tracker to help self-manage her moods and identify triggers to prevent a relapse, which helped her while trying to conceive and then when she found she was pregnant, tracking her moods helped her to manage her anxiety.

Marie worked with her healthcare team to put together a care plan so all her healthcare professionals could coordinate treatments.

At last, Marie gave birth to a perfect baby boy. She decided against breastfeeding, so she could go back on lithium. Her medications supported her to be the best mother she could be. Now her son is a happy, well-adjusted ten-year-old.

Marie's story is a perfect example of the need to work closely with healthcare professionals, even if you don't suffer from any complications. If you should require any medications, it can be complicated because pregnancy changes the way drugs are absorbed, distributed, metabolized, and excreted. In addition, after the thalidomide scandal of the 70s, it is important to be aware of the chances of a drug causing birth defects in the baby.

And this is the paradox of pregnancy. When it comes to taking meds when you're pregnant, less is more. The fewer drugs you take, the better. However, some pregnant women suffer from chronic conditions like hypertension or epilepsy, requiring medications. Some drugs used to treat these conditions are known to cause birth defects.

How do you reconcile the needs of the mother and the health of the baby?

It always has to be on a case by case basis, which is why you need to keep an open dialog with your healthcare team.

Most birth defects occur in the first trimester:

- 0-2 weeks are the formative weeks of rapid cell division, when it's all or nothing. Either the embryo fails to develop and dies, or it continues to grow. At this stage, it's impossible to know whether you're pregnant. This is why it's important to start thinking about your current medications and whether they're appropriate for pregnancy when trying to conceive, so you can change them before they can potentially cause any problems.
- 2-8 weeks is when most of the organs are forming. During this stage, many drugs and chemicals such as alcohol and tobacco can cause birth defects. You may know you're

pregnant by now, so if you are taking anything which is potentially harmful, stop as soon as possible, or at least start to cut back.

- 8 weeks and beyond is the period when most complications are either spontaneous abortion or developmental birth defects.

WHAT YOU CAN AND CAN'T TAKE WHEN YOU'RE EXPECTING

In 1979, the FDA introduced five categories of drugs (A, B, C, D, and X) to inform pregnant women and their caregivers about the relative risks of medications. These were replaced in 2015 after feedback that the letters were confusing and resulted in misunderstandings.

The new labeling makes it easier for women to make an informed decision about the medications they choose to take, although there is still no definitive 'yes' or 'no' surrounding most drugs. It is still crucial to seek input from clinicians to make a decision on a case-by-case basis as to whether the risk of side effects and harm to the baby outweighs the risk of side effects and harm to the mother. Many pregnant women require drug treatment for chronic conditions such as epilepsy, diabetes, hypertension or asthma. In addition, women are having babies at a later age, which also increases the chances of having a chronic condition.

Your healthcare provider will be able to advise you on whether a drug has no evidence of risk to the baby, such as levothyroxine, folic acid, liothyronine. They'll also tell you about drugs which have strong evidence of risk, such as thalidomide, and everything in between. It is then up to you whether you feel the benefits of a drug are worth the chances of harming the baby. For example, if you have cancer, most cancer drugs can harm the baby, but still need to be taken.

Other drugs, substances and food to avoid in pregnancy include:

> **NSAIDs** like ibuprofen and indomethacin in the third trimester of pregnancy. They can cause kidney damage to the baby as well as low levels of amniotic fluid[59] - the clear, slightly yellowish liquid that surrounds the unborn baby during pregnancy.
>
> **Alcohol** increases the risk of miscarriage, premature birth and low birthweight. It can also cause defects, such as fetal alcohol spectrum disorder[60].
>
> **Tobacco** has many negative effects on the baby (and mother). It can cause low birthweight and premature birth. Smoking can damage your baby's developing lungs and brains, damage which can linger through childhood and into teenage. It doubles the risk of abnormal bleeding during pregnancy and delivery, which is dangerous for both mother and child. It increases the risk of birth defects, such as cleft lip, and cleft palate. In addition, babies of mothers who smoke during pregnancy and beyond are at increased risk of SIDS (Sudden Infant Death Syndrome)[61].
>
> **Anticonvulsants** must be taken with care, since they are associated with birth defects and long term development[62].
>
> **Antibiotics** are generally safe, but some are associated with birth defects[63]. Always check the specific type of

antibiotics you've been prescribed to be sure that it's appropriate.

GO FOR THE SAFEST OPTIONS

If you are suffering a chronic condition, or develop a condition during pregnancy, look into all your options before deciding what to take. Don't be afraid to question your doctor about a specific drug. Read the information leaflet to be aware of possible side effects to watch out for. If you are taking medications and you notice anything out of the ordinary, check with your doctor if it's something to be concerned about. You may need to stop taking it or switch to an alternative.

Hypertension. If you suffer from hypertension or develop high blood pressure during pregnancy, you are most likely to be prescribed labetalol, nifedipine, or methyldopa. There's extensive evidence for the safety of these drugs for pregnant women.

Pain. If you need pain relief, you might want to look into natural forms of pain relief, such as warm baths, meditation, rest, rehydration, etc. If you really need to take something, you should be aware of the implications. As mentioned earlier, NSAIDs can be taken up to 20 weeks but should be avoided after this. Acetaminophen, which is the active ingredient in Tylenol, is generally considered to be safe. There is some evidence for a connection between taking it during pregnancy and ADHD or autism in children[64]. Aspirin can cause heavy bleeding in labor, so should be taken with caution during the final trimester. The most common form of prescription painkillers are opiates, which can potentially harm the baby and should only be prescribed when absolutely necessary[65].

Nausea and vomiting. Morning sickness is an unfortunate reality for many pregnant women. Since the thalidomide scandal, many women are naturally cautious about taking medication to treat their morning sickness. One natural remedy is ginger - you can safely drink up to four cups of ginger tea a day to treat your nausea. Cut back as you near your due date, since there is some evidence to show it increases the risk of bleeding. It should also be avoided if you have a history of miscarriage, vaginal bleeding, or blood clots[66]. If your morning sickness is more severe, then there are some drugs available which can help. Antihistamines have been shown to offer some relief, as has vitamin B6. However, if your morning sickness persists, you may have hyperemesis gravidarum, which may require IV fluids[67]. Don't be afraid to ask for help if you're struggling to cope with your nausea.

Diabetes. If you suffer from diabetes or develop gestational diabetes, help is at hand. The first thing to try is to change your diet to manage your blood sugar levels. If this isn't enough, insulin is the first drug of choice. It doesn't cross the placenta so won't hurt the baby. However, there are some oral options available, such as metformin, if insulin isn't suitable for whatever reason.

SUPPLEMENTS FOR A HEALTHY PREGNANCY

There are many supplements which are advised for pregnant women to take to support their health during this special time:

Calcium and magnesium sulfate. There is evidence to suggest that taking daily calcium supplements can reduce your risk of high blood pressure during pregnancy. However, the jury is out on the optimal dosage[68].

Folic acid (vitamin B9) and folinic acid (5-formyl tetrahydrofolate) have a number of health benefits. Folic acid is a synthetic form of folate while folinic acid occurs naturally in food. Folates are an important supplement for pregnant women to prevent serious birth defects like spina bifida and anencephaly[69].

Vitamin B complex is the collective term for B vitamins which are particularly important during pregnancy. Vitamins B6, B9, and B12 are especially connected with a reduced risk of birth defects, and may relieve some pregnancy symptoms as well as lower the chance of developing preeclampsia[70].

Omega 3 fatty acids are crucial building blocks of the fetal brain. They may also support the length of gestation and play a role in preventing perinatal depression. They are mainly derived from seafood and algae. Since most Americans don't consume much seafood, taking supplements during pregnancy is important to maintain levels of this powerful substance[71].

Pregnancy is just nine months long, but there are times when it feels like it's going to go on forever. Longer, even, especially if you're unfortunate enough to suffer from some of the negative pregnancy symptoms like prolonged morning sickness or swollen ankles. When your baby is in your arms, it's all worth it, but there may be times when you feel like it'll never happen.

There's a lot of support and help available for anything you may experience during pregnancy. Just remember to always double check whether something you want to take is safe for pregnant women. If in doubt, ask your healthcare professional to see if something is suitable for you, whether it's an over-the-counter medication, prescription medicine, or a home remedy.

Of course, once your pregnancy is over, you've then got two people's health to worry about! In the next chapter, we'll look at what you need to consider when it comes to caring for your child's health.

11

CARING FOR KIDS

Treating Kids' Health Problems Safely

Among the most sacred gifts you can give your child is the gift of health. This gift is best given by example.

– Dr. Rand Olson

The woman jiggling a baby in a stroller looked like she hadn't slept in a week. Her hair was barely brushed, her clothes disheveled and she was wearing odd socks.

"You've got to help me," she pleaded. "She just won't stop crying. The doctor says she's got colic, and there's not a lot I can do, but there has to be *something*."

As if on cue, the baby started wailing. The woman stuck a pacifier in its mouth, but it kept screaming.

And then she said something which sent a shiver down my spine.

"It's gotten so bad I've been giving her children's Tylenol before every feed, just to try and calm her down. It's the only way I can get some sleep!"

How could I break it to her that she was potentially causing her baby long term harm? An overdose of Tylenol can lead to liver damage and even death.

"Okay," I said. "Let's go over a few things. Do you breast or bottle feed?"

"Bottle feed."

"Have you tried this brand? It's got a good reputation for helping colicky babies." I went and got a tub of a recommended brand of formula.

"No, I haven't," said the woman.

"Try that. I've also got some gas drops you can give her instead of Tylenol. Tylenol won't help and it could make things worse. Maybe have a break from that."

"Really?"

"I'd advise keeping Tylenol to a minimum if you can," I said gently. "It does carry some risks and it's not recommended as a treatment for colic."

Her shoulders sagged. "It's the only thing that seemed to help and I'm just so *tired*."

"I understand. These early months are tough - I've got kids of my own, so I've been there. It does get better though. Switch formula and see how she gets on with the gas drops." I smiled at her. "Oh and you might like to try swaddling her. Some babies prefer that. And if you can afford it, try a white noise machine. And if you can't afford it, just have the vacuum running in the background."

"The vacuum? Seriously?"

"Seriously! Some people swear by it to soothe a cranky baby."

"Well then, I guess I'll give it a go. Anything's got to be better than listening to her crying all the time."

She smiled weakly, paid for the formula and gas drops. I never saw her again, so I have no idea if it worked, but I like to feel that the reason she didn't return was because her baby finally got the relief she needed. I really sympathized - my oldest son suffered from colic as well, and I knew first hand how hard it was to hold a screaming baby knowing there was nothing you could do to soothe them.

I hate to break it to you, but the moment your baby is born, you're in for a lifetime of worry. You stress about whether your child is hitting their milestones, whether that sneeze is something more serious, whether they'll get into the right school, whether they'll be successful, whether they'll want to look after you in their old age...

SUPPORTING YOUR CHILD'S HEALTH WITH IMMUNIZATIONS

According to the American Academy of Pediatrics, immunizations are a major public health achievement and are a safe, effective way to protect children from disease, disability, and even death.

Immunizations have also been the cause of some controversy, with side effects allegedly including anything from autism[72] and asthma[73] through to disability[74] and in some very rare cases death[75].

It's difficult to know the best thing to do when there are so many conflicting sources of information out there.

The best thing to do if you have any doubts is to speak to your pediatrician in the first instance. They will be able to talk you through the pros and cons of each immunization, so you can make your mind up over whether your child needs each one. If there is a family history of adverse reactions to immunizations or any of the ingredients in them, they'll be able to advise you on the risks vs benefits. If you have concerns over the immunization schedule, they can help you modify it to space out when the jabs are given, which some people believe minimizes the risk of side effects.

They can also point you in the direction of reliable sources of information - remember, just because it's on the internet doesn't make it true! And bear in mind that the overwhelming majority of children are immunized without any ill effects whatsoever.

SUPPLEMENTS FOR CHILDREN

A healthy diet is one of the most important ways to raise a healthy child. Children need a broad range of vitamins and minerals for proper development, and the best way to get these is directly from food.

- Try to feed your child at least five portions of fruit and vegetables a day, as well as whole grains and proteins. Some children are fussier than others, so you might look into things like hiding fruit and veg in smoothies. Get your child involved in preparing their own food in an age appropriate manner. It's amazing the difference a little autonomy can make to a picky eater.

- Limit red meat (beef, pork, and lamb) and avoid processed meats like bacon, sausages, hot dogs, deli meats, etc. In fact, try to avoid processed food in general.

- Fat is an essential part of a healthy diet, but it's important to consume the right kinds of fat. Try to provide healthy unsaturated fats from fish, nuts, seeds, plants, etc. Restrict foods high in saturated fat, particularly red meat, and avoid unhealthy trans fats found in partially hydrogenated oils.

- Milk and dairy products are a good source of calcium and vitamin D. Try to give unflavored milk, plain yogurt, and other unsweetened dairy foods with just a little bit of cheese.

- Water is always better than juice, which should be confined to mealtimes if given at all.

With the best will in the world, some children are picky eaters and will turn their nose up at healthy food in favor of junk food. It's very easy to give them what they want just so they'll eat *something*. If you've got a child which refuses to eat healthily, supplements can help compensate for a suboptimal diet.

Children are most commonly deficient in:

Vitamin D, which can lead to rickets and bone disease.

Vitamin B12, which can lead to a type of anemia. If you are bringing your child up to be vegetarian or vegan, they may not get enough B12 from diet alone.

Calcium, which can lead to rickets, osteoporosis, and osteopenia.

Iodine, which can cause goiter and intellectual disabilities.

Iron deficiency might be a problem if your child is vegan or vegetarian, eats a restricted diet, has celiac disease or gastrointestinal blood loss. This can make it more likely for your child to get sick or develop an infection.

Zinc may also be an issue with a vegan or vegetarian diet, which can slow down growth.

The problem with just taking supplements to counteract these deficiencies is that supplements can be harmful in the wrong dose. In fact, they could be more dangerous than looking for alternative food types to give your child a particular vitamin or mineral. For example, iron poisoning can corrode the intestinal lining. If an overdose is left untreated, it can result in death.

Before giving your child any supplements, consult an appropriate healthcare professional, such as your doctor or pharmacist. They'll be able to advise you on the best supplement for your child's age and situation.

HEALTH PROBLEMS IN CHILDREN

While it can be tempting to turn to Dr. Google for advice if your child is unwell, he is not a reliable source! Don't try to self-diagnose your child's symptoms - many rashes look similar, for example, but some are no cause for concern while others can be symptomatic of life-threatening conditions. Dr. Google will throw you into a panic for the slightest sniffle, so do your nerves a favor and go to a proper doctor with an actual medical degree!

Pharmacists are also a good source of information on how to treat minor childhood ailments and conditions. They'll be able to let you know whether you should make an appointment with a pediatrician or provide information on appropriate medications.

REMEMBER TO ASK FOR HELP

We covered this in chapter 2, but it's just as important to use HELP with any medications given to your child.

> **H** - "How many" pills have you been given? Do you have enough for your child's course of treatment? For example, if they need one pill three times a day for two weeks, you'll need 42 pills.
>
> **E** - When are your pills "expiring"? Don't be tempted to hoard your child's medication in case they get sick again. All medications have an expiry date, and it can be dangerous to take out of date drugs. Take any past their use by date back to the pharmacy for appropriate disposal.
>
> **L** - What is the "label" of your meds? Familiarize yourself with the generic name of your child's tablets, so you can tell your physician about any side effects and whether another brand is better for your child.
>
> **P** - When you fill your prescription, double check that what you've been given matches what you've been prescribed. Notify your pharmacist of any discrepancies - it's especially important that children are given the right medication because their bodies have different needs to an adult's.

Note that infants and toddlers are usually given syrups or injectables because they may choke on tablets. Keep all medications out of the reach of children, ideally locked away, until the time comes for them to take their dose. Some children's medications are deliberately sweetened to make them more palatable, but sometimes they taste *too* nice, so children will want more. They can accidentally overdose if they've been helping themselves.

If your child has been given an inhaler or needs injecting, e.g. with insulin, ask your doctor or pharmacist to show you exactly how to administer the medication.

DRUGS TO AVOID IN CHILDREN

Do not be tempted to give your child any of your medication if they're unwell. Children's bodies metabolize drugs differently, and what can be amazing for an adult can be lethal for a child.

These are some of the most common drugs you should avoid giving your child. If in doubt, ask a doctor or pharmacist before giving any medications.

> **Aspirin.** This common pain reliever can cause Reye's syndrome in children, which causes fat to build up around the brain, liver, and other organs, potentially with lethal effect. The risk is highest if your child is suffering from a virus like chickenpox or flu, but it's still never a good idea to dispense aspirin to your child unless under doctor's orders. Always check labels carefully and ask your pharmacist if a drug is safe for a child, since many combination drugs include aspirin.
>
> **Cough and cold remedies.** Over-the-counter cough and cold medicines do not work on children younger than 6. (And to be honest, have minimal effect on anyone older than that.)[76] Worse, they can have some serious side

effects, including allergic reactions, neurological problems, and even death.

Iron supplements. We've discussed this before, but I wanted to mention it again because iron poisoning is the most common form of poisoning in children under 6[77]. If you feel your child is iron deficient, discuss with your pediatrician before giving any supplements. Keep iron tablets in child-proof bottles safely locked away.

Bismuth Subsalicylate. You may be more familiar with this as Pepto Bismol. It's a common remedy for upset tummies. However, it's been linked to Reye's Syndrome in children under 12. If your child is suffering from heartburn, gas, or diarrhea, talk to your doctor or pharmacist about safer alternatives. Often, these problems go away by themselves or with a change in diet.

If your child throws up or develops a rash after taking any drug, call your doctor. If they accidentally overdose on a medication, call for emergency help or go to the emergency room, especially if they're struggling to breathe, have passed out, are twitching or behaving strangely.

Being a parent is a lifelong responsibility. Caring for your child's health is one of the most important jobs you'll ever have. I'll admit that there've been times I've felt so worried and stressed about my children that I've found it hard to breathe.

Speaking of which, next we'll be looking at respiratory problems ...

12

COUGHING & SNEEZING

The Causes & Treatments For The Sniffles

Coughing in the theater is not a respiratory ailment. It is a criticism.

– Alan Jay Lerner

I knew Mrs. Adams (not her real name) well. She'd been on high dose steroids and antibiotics for three months now and she was regularly coming in to the pharmacy for repeat prescriptions. She loved a good chat, but she always struggled to draw breath while she spoke.

"How are you doing today, Mrs. Adams?" I asked.

"Not good." She sighed, but it quickly became a hacking cough which lingered too long for my liking. "I'm sure this cough is really pneumonia. I think I need to go back to the doctor and get him to give me stronger drugs. I've asked before but he's told me it's nothing to worry about. A cough like this can't be nothing, can it?" She started coughing again.

"Maybe." I thought for a moment. "Have you considered seeing a respiratory specialist?"

"What would they do? I just need drugs."

"Sure, drugs might be what you need, but maybe there's another way of helping you with your cough. A specialist will be able to support you to put together the right treatment plan. It's just a thought." I filled out her prescription and Mrs. Adams left the pharmacy, still coughing.

It was a few weeks before she returned to the pharmacy. She was a completely different woman. She had a spring in her step and there was no sign of a cough.

"You're looking well, Mrs. Adams," I said.

"I *feel* well." She beamed and her smile lit up the room. "I took your advice and asked to see a respiratory specialist. It turned out that the steroids I was taking were causing my cough! I never would have believed it if you hadn't told me to go to the specialist. He's helped me come up with a plan to stop taking them and I'm only on a small dose now. In a couple of weeks I'll stop taking them completely."

"That's great news!"

"'The specialist also taught me a few breathing techniques and they've really helped me. I'm hardly wheezing anymore. He showed me how to use my inhaler properly. Turns out I've been doing it wrong all this time! I've got a peak flow meter and chart so I know when to call for help. It's changed my life - and it's all thanks to your advice."

COUGHS AND SNEEZES SPREAD DISEASES

We all suffer from coughs and sneezes from time to time. Children frequently pick up coughs and colds from kindergarten or school. Then they bring them home to share with the rest of the family. How generous of them.

A sneeze is when you experience a sudden expulsion of air from the lungs. This travels quickly through the nose and mouth to send out droplets of mucus, spreading infection. In comparison, a cough can be voluntary or involuntary. It is a reflex action which clears your airways of any mucus or irritants.

There are many different types of cough. Some are more serious than others:

Dry cough. These coughs are described as 'unproductive' because nothing comes up when you cough. They sound dry. These are usually the least serious, although they sometimes may interrupt sleep, or give you a headache or sore throat. They usually go away by themselves.

Wet cough. These coughs usually bring up mucus. They are the body's way of getting rid of excess mucus caused by an infection. They may also be caused by COPD (chronic obstructive pulmonary disease). Since they are typically caused by an infection, they may require medication.

Croup. More common in children than adults, croup causes a barking sound when you cough. The virus that causes croup often also brings on a raspy voice, breathing difficulties, and/or fever. The best thing to do when you have croup is to sit in a steamy bathroom. This will help open up the airways. If you have concerns about your child's ability to breathe when they have croup, take them to the doctor.

Uncontrollable or paroxysmal coughing. These coughs are violent, and painful. Whooping cough is a form of uncontrollable coughing and is the most serious. Also known as the 'Three Month Cough' because of how long it takes to recover, whooping cough causes deep coughing which is worse at night. Coughs are followed by a deep inhale with the distinctive whoop sound which gives the cough its name. Whooping cough can cause oxygen deprivation because it's hard to breathe when caught up in a coughing fit. If you suspect whooping cough, go to your doctor for confirmation and treatment.

HOW LONG WILL MY COUGH LAST?

There are three different types of coughs in terms of duration:

Acute coughs. These last up to three weeks and are usually caused by a virus. While it's natural to want to take something to relieve your cough, studies have shown existing treatments for acute coughs to be ineffective[78]. Unless the cough is causing other issues, it's better to let it run its course. Alternatively, if the cough is the result of an underlying bacterial infection, such as pneumonia, a course of antibiotics is the most effective treatment. Speak to your healthcare provider about the best course of action.

Subacute coughs. These last between 3-8 weeks. While a subacute cough may go away by itself, it's best to get yourself checked out by a healthcare provider if you've been coughing for over three weeks.

Chronic coughs. These last over eight weeks. By this time, you should have sought medical advice. If not, don't delay any further. The cause of a chronic cough can be difficult to determine. Your healthcare provider may need to run a number of tests or refer you to a specialist.

THE CAUSES OF COUGHS AND SNEEZES

There are many different reasons why you may cough or sneeze. Some are more serious than others. The most common causes include:

Infections. These may range from the relatively benign, such as a cold, or more serious conditions such as pneumonia, tuberculosis (TB), influenza (flu) or COVID. If you have any concerns about your cough, consult your healthcare practitioner.

Allergies. Allergens like grass and tree pollen, mold and fungi spores, dust, and animal dander can irritate the nasal lining, causing post nasal drip. This means that watery mucus is dripping down from the nose and into the throat, which becomes aggravated, resulting in a cough. There are a range of treatments available to help the symptoms of allergies. Speak to your healthcare practitioner to discuss the best one for you.

Build up of fluid in the lungs. There are a number of reasons why you might experience this, such as pneumonia, cancer, or heart, liver, or kidney disease. If this is the cause of your cough, you will need to work with your healthcare team to deal with the underlying issue.

Irritation of the respiratory tract. This may be due to an infection. It may also result from being exposed to toxins, pollutants, irritants, and allergens. One of the biggest causes of a chronic cough is smoking[79], which irritates the respiratory tract (among other things). The most effective treatment for a smoker's cough is to stop smoking. I know this is much easier said than done, but there is help available to support you to quit. Speak to your healthcare provider to learn more about your options.

Drugs. Many medications can cause respiratory issues. Paracetamol and aspirin can induce asthma[80]. Narcotics and other recreational drugs may depress respiration and bring on a coughing fit. Alcohol abuse can damage the lungs and increase your risk of developing conditions like pneumonia[81]. Sleeping pills can interfere with your normal breathing[82]. Check to see whether coughing is listed as a side effect of your medication. If you suspect it is making you cough, consult your healthcare provider about alternatives.

HOW TO NURSE YOURSELF THROUGH A COUGH OR COLD

Frustratingly, for all our medical advances, we still don't have a cure for the common cold. The best treatment is time, but it can be really miserable suffering while you wait for your cough to go away. There are a few things you can do to nurse yourself through a cough or cold:

- Rest up and drink plenty of fluids. (Preferably hot drinks[83].)
- Take vitamin supplements, especially vitamin C[84].
- Take any medications as prescribed by your doctor or pharmacist.
- Cough into your elbow and self-isolate to minimize the risk of spreading infection.

- Avoid recreational drugs, tobacco, and alcohol. If you've been prescribed sleeping pills, discuss with your doctor whether you should take them while you're suffering from respiratory problems.

- If you notice your cough getting worse, it lasts for over two weeks, you have problems breathing, a fever, or you see blood in your sputum (saliva and mucus), consult a doctor immediately. These may be an indicator of a more serious underlying condition.

While it's no fun to be coughing, it's worth bearing in mind that most coughs aren't a sign of anything serious. Take it as an opportunity to put your feet up for a few days!

In the next chapter, we'll be looking at various skin diseases, what causes them, and what you can do to have healthy looking skin.

13

YOUR LARGEST ORGAN - SKIN

Simple Tips For Healthy Skin

"Real skin has texture, pores, and even the occasional blemish. The goal is healthy skin, not perfect skin"

– Sean Garrette

As the man reached out for the tub of skin cream, I could see how red and irritated his hands were.

"Is this cream any good?" he asked me, placing it on the counter.

"It depends," I replied. "What's the problem?"

"I've had terrible dermatitis for months. It started off with a bit of redness, but it's gotten worse and worse. My hands are cracked and the skin's peeling off. The itching and pain is so bad it wakes me up at night. I've had to take so much time off work. I hate feeling useless, but my hands just won't let me do my job."

"What do you do?"

"I'm a tiler. And don't tell me to try wearing gloves - I have. But I do highly skilled, intricate work and you can't wear gloves for that."

I smiled. "I wasn't going to do that. But I do wonder whether you've had yourself tested for allergies?"

The man frowned. "I didn't think allergies could do something like this. I thought they made you sneeze."

"It depends," I told him. "They can also cause contact dermatitis. If the skin creams aren't helping, they could actually be damaging your skin."

"Oh." The man looked at his hands with a worried frown. "I guess I won't be needing this after all." He left the skin cream on the counter and left.

A few weeks later, I happened to bump into the man at the store. A huge grin spread across his face when he saw me. He lifted up his hands and waved them at me. While they still had a reddish tinge, they looked so much better than when I'd last seen him.

"I got myself referred to a skin specialist," he explained. "They tested me and found that I've got allergies to cement and the chemicals in rubber gloves. No wonder my hands were sore! I've been working with my specialist to find ways of avoiding my triggers and improve my dermatitis. I tell you something - if you ever need some tiling, give me a call and I'll do it for free!"

Skin conditions are incredibly common, with as many as one in three Americans suffering from some form of skin disease[85]. Chronic skin conditions aren't just physically debilitating. It's also widely recognized that they have a negative impact on sufferers' self-esteem and confidence[86]. People with visible skin problems may become withdrawn, avoid social situations, or change the way they dress to compensate for their appearance. They may feel embarrassed or distressed. To compound the issue, the modern preoccupation with self-image and the prevalence of social media places even more pressure on people with skin problems.

There are many different types of skin diseases. It's important you don't turn to Dr. Google to diagnose any rashes you may develop. It's difficult to tell the difference between similar looking conditions from photos online. A qualified professional will be able to let you know whether a rash is a mild case of temporary contact dermatitis or something more serious like cancer.

Some of the most common skin diseases include:

Eczema. This is an inflammatory skin condition. Symptoms include itchiness, dry skin, rashes, scaly patches, blisters, and infections. There are seven different types of eczema and over 31 million Americans suffer from it[87]. It can develop at any age, from newborn to adulthood. It can go through phases when the symptoms worsen. This is known as a 'flare-up.' Treatments can include moisturizers, antihistamines, steroid creams and corticosteroids.

Psoriasis. Over 7.5 million American adults suffer from this skin condition[88]. It is caused by a dysfunction of the immune system which causes inflammation in the body. This may cause visible symptoms, such as raised plaques and scales on the skin. Some people find that these plaques itch, burn, or sting. Psoriasis can strike at any age, although it's most common between the ages of 15-25. Treatments include topical treatments, light therapy (phototherapy), prescription medication and complementary and integrative medicine.

Acne. The bane of teenagers the world over, the main symptom of acne is spots across the face, back and chest. It may also make the skin oily, hot or painful to touch. It is caused by blocked hair follicles, tiny holes in the skin. This happens when the sebaceous glands, which lubricate the hair and skin, produce too much sebum. This sebum mixes with dead skin cells which then clog the follicle. The sebaceous glands are sensitive to hormones, which is why teenage acne is so prevalent. The surge in hormones during this time contributes to the rise in sebum. Women are more likely to have adult acne than men due to hormonal changes during periods and pregnancy. Other triggers include makeup, certain medications, and smoking. Treatments vary according to the individual patient and it can take a few months before symptoms improve. Prescription medications may be required for more persistent, serious acne. UV light therapy is another option, although it is becoming less popular since it is associated with an increased risk of cancer and there isn't enough evidence to support its effectiveness.

Skin infections. These are caused when germs (bacteria, viruses, or fungi), yeast, or parasites infect the skin and sometimes the deep tissues beneath it. Common infections include:

- Cellulitis (when bacteria get into the deep tissues of the skin)
- Erysipelas (an infection of the upper layers of the skin)
- Impetigo (a contagious bacterial infection causing sores and blisters)
- Folliculitis (when hair follicles become inflamed)
- Furuncles (boils) and carbuncles (clusters of boils).

The cause of the infection will determine the most appropriate treatment, which could include, amongst others: antibiotics, antifungals or antivirals.

CARING FOR YOUR SKIN

There's a lot you can do for yourself to keep your skin looking healthy:

- Wash your face twice a day using non-medicated soap unless prescribed by your doctor.

- Keep shaving to the bare minimum.

- Bathe regularly. If you have sensitive skin, make sure you treat the water before soaking in it.

- If you have allergies, like our friend at the start of this chapter, avoid known triggers as much as possible. You may want to get yourself diagnosed by a specialist, or you could simply observe when you have a reaction and note what you were exposed to just before.

- Moisturize regularly and use plenty of sunscreen.

- Choose your skincare products carefully. Avoid oily creams which may exacerbate acne and use ones suited to your skin type.

- Do not bleach your skin. Too much chlorine in your bloodstream can be toxic, and it's also possible to have an allergic reaction to bleach. Leave your skin the beautiful color it was born to be.

- Do not blend medicated products into your creams. You have no means of measuring dosage or predicting side effects.

- Eat a balanced, low-sugar diet. Although the evidence is inconclusive about the impact of diet on skin condition, many believe that the state of the skin is a reflection of your gut health. (We'll go more into this in a later chapter.) If you are allergic to a food type, it may cause a rash. And

- even if it doesn't make any difference to your skin, it's always good to have a healthy diet!

- Use makeup minimally. While there's a lot of societal pressure on us to look our best at all times, makeup could be making your skin worse. Using it to cover up blemishes becomes a vicious cycle as the 'cure' turns out to be causing the problems. If you can, try to have at least one or two makeup free days a week.

If you have any concerns about your skin, speak to your healthcare providers. They will be able to diagnose the exact cause of the problem and put together an appropriate treatment plan for you.

We've touched upon skin infections in this chapter. In the next chapter, we'll look more deeply into the subject of infections, what causes them, how you can treat them and how to make sure you're getting the right treatment.

Your Workbook includes a helpful allergen tracker. With this, you'll have a smart way to determine what may be causing any skin problems you experience which means you may prevent a prolonged search for a cure.

www.learnwellbooks.com/healthy

14

INFECTIONS

The 8 Main Types & How To Treat Them

I almost had to have my leg amputated because of an infection.

– Dick Dale

FOR EXCELLENT HEALTH DO THIS

After I graduated, I spent some time volunteering in India. I wanted to see something of the world before I returned home to settle down. My pharmacy skills meant I could do something to help people while I explored other cultures.

I had an amazing time during my three years in India. I made many friends for life and the hands-on experience I got was invaluable after college.

I remember one of my friends, Tom, was working as a medical intern. We often had lunch together and one day he showed up with a large bandaid on his index finger.

"What happened?" I asked.

"Oh, I was doing a lumbar puncture on an HIV-infected patient and I managed to catch myself with the needle."

"That's not good. Are you okay?"

"There was a little bleeding, but not much. I cleaned the wound immediately and they gave me antiretrovirals. They've also given me a rapid HIV test and I should get the results soon."

Tom was remarkably calm given the circumstances, but then he was used to working long hours under pressure. To him, this was a risk that came with the job. His brother had died from AIDS, so he had a particular interest in helping others suffering from the HIV virus.

Luckily, his test came back negative, but two weeks later, his finger was still swollen.

"You should get that checked out," I advised him as we sat down to eat our sandwiches together.

"I know, I know. I've just been too busy to find the time."

"Come on," I told him, getting up and gesturing to him. "Let's go and get it tested now. Then you know it's done."

"All right." Tom sighed as the pair of us went to find a doctor who would be able to check out his finger. As it turned out, he needed a local anesthetic to remove a sample of pus for testing before draining the wound. A sample of it showed that he'd been infected by *Staphylococcus aureus,* a type of bacteria. He was immediately started on antibiotics.

As a medical professional himself, Tom was cleaning and dressing his wound every day, but it simply wasn't healing. He was put on a wide range of different antibiotics, but none of them made any difference.

For the next six months, his finger continued to swell and the swelling seemed to spread to his hand. He suffered from a low-grade fever and night sweats, and he was losing weight. He underwent a surgical debridement to remove any dead, damaged, or infected tissue, but his condition still failed to improve.

Ten months later, he had another surgical debridement and this time he finally got the answers to his health problems. A culture of the removed tissue showed that he had cutaneous tuberculosis - TB in the skin.

Now that he had a diagnosis, Tom was started on a 6 month course of anti-TB drugs and given another HIV test, just in case. He quickly saw an improvement in his condition and by the end of his treatment, he'd fully recovered. His HIV test came back negative.

Even medical professionals can overlook symptoms that indicate infection. Such a mistake can lead to consequences far worse than early, appropriate intervention. Make sure you act when presented with symptoms. Even if that only amounts to negative test results.

THE EIGHT MAIN CAUSES OF INFECTION

Infections can be relatively benign, but if left untreated, they can rapidly descend into something more serious. There are eight main causes of infection:

> **Virus** (e.g. AIDS, COVID, Hepatitis B, herpes, etc.)
>
> **Bacteria** (e.g. gonorrhea, tuberculosis, leprosy, chlamydia, etc.)
>
> **Fungus** (e.g. candidiasis, cryptococcosis, pneumocystis pneumonia, blastomycosis, etc.)
>
> **Rickettsia** (A genus of obligate intracellular bacteria which cause rickettsiosis. Most Rickettsioses are transmitted by ticks, but they may also be spread by fleas, lice, and mites.)
>
> **Prions** (Misfolded proteins which can transmit their damaged shape onto normal forms of the same protein. They can be responsible for many fatal and transmissible neurodegenerative diseases such as Mad Cow disease.)

Protozoa (Single celled organisms which cause diseases like malaria, sleeping sickness, amoebiasis, etc.)

Filarial worms (Roundwords, tapeworms, etc.)

Mites and lice (Technically, these cause infestations rather than infections, e.g. scabies.)

Infections may occur anywhere in the body - the bones, kidney, heart, brain, eyes, stomach, skin, etc. Where the infection occurs combined with its cause will determine the type of infection someone is suffering from. For example, the layers around the brain and spinal cord are known as 'meninges' and may be infected with bacteria, viruses, or fungi. This causes them to become swollen and inflamed - meningitis. Symptoms are very serious, including fever, severe headache, and a rash that doesn't disappear when a glass is pressed against it. Left untreated, it can cause death, which may occur quickly, especially in children. It can usually be effectively treated with antibiotics, so if you or your loved ones experience any of these symptoms, especially the rash, seek medical advice immediately.

HOW TO TREAT AN INFECTION

Never attempt to diagnose or treat an infection by yourself. You may be contributing to the problem of drug resistance. This is when a drug becomes less effective due to the organisms it targets having developed resistance. This is known to be a particular problem with antibiotics when they've been over-prescribed or taken unnecessarily, such as to treat a virus, which cannot be dealt with by antibiotics. There is growing concern over the abuse of antibiotics in livestock farming. In the European

Union, livestock is given over three times the amount dispensed to humans which has resulted in super-resistant bacteria.

This is why it's so important to seek a diagnosis from a qualified professional. Then, you should take the drugs exactly as prescribed so they can do their job.

> **Antibiotics** are used to treat bacterial infections. Since they were first introduced in the 1940s they have saved millions of lives. Their efficacy is now under threat due to drug resistant bacteria. They work by blocking essential processes in bacteria, killing them or preventing them from multiplying so the immune system can fight off the infection. Different antibiotics work with different bacteria. Broad spectrum antibiotics such as amoxicillin and gentamicin affect a wide range of bacteria. Narrow spectrum antibiotics such as spectrum only affect a few types.
>
> Your doctor will choose the right antibiotic to treat the type of bacteria causing your infection. This may require a test. Be aware of the active ingredient in your antibiotic so you can let your doctor know if you may be allergic. Up to 10% of people suffer from the most common side effects of antibiotics, including stomach problems and thrush infections[89]. Less common side effects include allergic reactions or ongoing diarrhea from an intestinal infection.
>
> Discuss with your doctor or pharmacist the possible side effects so you can determine whether the benefits are greater than the risk. Also ask whether there are any medications you should not take with your antibiotic.

Antivirals are used to treat viral infections. They work differently according to the virus and drug type. They may block receptors so viruses can't bind to or enter healthy cells; boost the immune system so it can fight off the infection; or lower the amount of active virus/viral load in the body. This can ease symptoms and make you feel better faster. In some cases, antivirals can eliminate the virus. Other chronic conditions, like HIV, hepatitis, and herpes, cannot be cured with antivirals. Instead, they may make the virus inactive, meaning you have few, if any, symptoms. Taking antivirals may also lower the risk of you passing on a virus or getting infected in the first place.

Antivirals are usually taken orally, but they're also available as eye drops, in powder form, as ointments or creams, or injected into a muscle or vein. The treatment length will depend on the infection and drug. You may only need one dose of an IV drug or a week of pills to treat an acute infection. If you have a chronic illness, you may have to take antivirals for life.

Side effects can include a cough, dry mouth, diarrhea, dizziness, fatigue, headaches, insomnia, joint or muscle pain, or a rash. However, generally speaking, antivirals are safe and may be taken by babies from the age of two weeks as well as pregnant and breastfeeding women. Discuss with your healthcare provider whether an antiviral is appropriate for you.

Antifungals treat fungal infections and are often available without prescription. They may be given as a cream, gel, ointment, spray, oral medication, injection, or pessary.

They work by either killing the fungus or stopping it from growing.

Before you start taking an antifungal, speak to your pharmacist or doctor about any existing conditions or allergies so they can prescribe the right one. They should tell you whether it may interact with your other medications and if it's suitable to take while pregnant or breastfeeding. (Many aren't.) They will also be able to talk you through potential side effects.

Most side effects are mild and do not last long. They may include itching or burning, redness or a rash, nausea, or diarrhea. In rare cases you may have an allergic reaction, severe skin reaction or liver damage. It is important you seek medical advice if you notice any signs of these, such as jaundice, vomiting, difficulties breathing, dark pee or pale poo, or peeling or blistering skin.

Prion protein-lowering treatments may slow the progress of a disease caused by prions. Unfortunately, at the time of writing, there is no known cure for these infections. Your healthcare team will focus on keeping you as safe and comfortable as possible, so you should carry out a risk/benefit analysis with them.

Antiprotozoals treat infections caused by protozoa, single-cell parasites. They are available as tablets and capsules, as well as in powder form to create an injectable solution.

They may destroy the protozoa or hinder their ability to grow and reproduce. They can damage the protozoal DNA to slow infection. They also inhibit the metabolism of the protozoa so they can't grow or reproduce.

As with all drugs, antiprotozoals come with potential side effects. The most common include diarrhea, nausea, vomiting, abdominal pain, or loss of appetite, Rare side effects include anemia, low white blood cell count, low blood platelet count, high blood pressure, heart damage, nerve pain, encephalopathy (brain damage), shock, damage to the eyes, or damage to the kidneys. Discuss with your doctor whether an antiprotozoal is the best treatment for you.

Deworming. There are hundreds of different types of worms which target humans. WHO recommends periodic deworming in areas where worms are endemic[90]. Deworming medication will kill adult worms in the intestines but won't harm any eggs or immature worms. This is why repeating the dose every six months may be necessary. You should treat the whole family at the same time and potentially two weeks after initial treatment if a second dose is required. Existing worm eggs will cause a reinfection, as will ingesting more eggs.

Good hygiene will help prevent (re)infection. Wash your hands before preparing food and after handling soil or going to the toilet. Deworm your pet dog or cat regularly. Thoroughly wash any garden grown fruit or vegetables and if you live in a high risk area drink bottled water.

Dewormers are generally safe. Mild side effects may occur, such as dizziness, nausea, diarrhea, or headache. Consult a medical professional if these persist past 24 hours or are severe. If you have liver problems, are pregnant or breastfeeding, or taking any medications, it's important to inform your doctor before taking dewormers. These may impact your treatment.

Pediculicides are medications which treat lice. However, the best treatment for lice (and best prevention too!) is good hygiene. Regularly change and clean your clothes and bedding. Shower or bathe frequently. While it is a myth that head lice only target children with dirty hair, washing bedding following an infestation will prevent reinfestation.

Lice spread through close contact with someone who is infested, which is why children often get head lice. Treating the whole family may be necessary if you notice a lice infestation. However, do not give pediculicides 'just in case' - lotions and sprays do not prevent an infestation. You'll be unnecessarily exposing yourself or your family to harsh chemicals.

SAFETY TIPS WHEN TREATING AN INFECTION

- Always tell your doctor or pharmacist if you are pregnant, breastfeeding, or trying to conceive. Some antibiotics are unsuitable for pregnant or nursing women, so it's important to be sure you're taking one which is safe.

- Never self-medicate. You may end up making things worse. While there are complementary therapies which claim to treat infections, evidence for their efficacy is slim.

- Check that a medication is suitable for children if your child suffers an infection. For example, tetracycline is used to treat a wide range of infections, but should not be given to children under 8 years of age.

- Do not drink milk, grapefruit juice, or sweet drinks while on a course of antibiotics. They can decrease their effectiveness while increasing the risk of side effects[91].

- Always tell your doctor and pharmacist about any medications you're already taking. They may have an effect on your treatment.

- Ask about the symptoms to look out for which may indicate a serious adverse effect. If you notice anything untoward, tell your doctor immediately.

- Remember that in an ideal world you should be optimizing your medications to use the minimum amount of drugs to treat your condition. It may not always be necessary to treat an infection since the body's immune system may be able to fight it off. Check whether a drug is essential with your doctor or pharmacist.

A healthy immune system is one of the best ways to fight off an infection. The importance of good gut health is becoming increasingly recognised as the foundation of good health in general. In the next chapter, we'll look at how you can improve your gut health so if an infection hits your body has a fighting chance against it.

15

GUT HEALTH

4 Simple Steps To Combat Gut Health Issues

Let food be thy medicine.

– Hippocrates

"How is Katy doing?" I asked her mother when she came in to pick up her prescription. A regular visitor to the pharmacy, Beth loved to chat and I was very familiar with what had been going on with her family - good *and* bad.

In the case of her daughter Katy, it hadn't been good. She'd been a perfectly normal 14-year old girl. She was a member of her school Glee club and straight B student. About a year ago, she'd started having digestive problems.

Her behavior changed. The good student transformed into a teenager who was apathetic about her school work, bursting into tears for no good reason. Just a typical teen, you might think, but Beth insisted there was more to it than hormones.

Katy started complaining about severe headaches and insomnia. She lost weight and became extremely constipated, but worse was to come. She started having vivid hallucinations, hallucinations which seemed so real she genuinely thought they were happening. She'd think she'd heard her boyfriend or sister talking negatively about her or having arguments when her boyfriend wasn't even in the house. She'd be watching TV when suddenly the characters on the screen would climb out and chase after her.

"She's doing really well." Beth beamed and I could tell she wasn't just saying it because she didn't want to discuss her daughter. "After all those months of doctors telling us nothing was wrong or she just needed antidepressants, we took your advice and had her tested for celiac disease. Our doctor said we were wasting our money, but we went to a nutritionist who helped us with a gluten-free diet. Not only did it fix all Katy's digestive problems and stopped her losing anymore weight, the hallucinations went away! The doctor insisted on testing her with different flours because they couldn't believe a change in diet would make such a difference. They gave her bread from wheat flour and bread from rice flour. When she ate the gluten, all her symptoms came flooding back. When she ate the rice flour bread, it had no effect at all."

"That's amazing." My smile echoed Beth's.

"I've got my little girl back and it's all down to her diet. Who'd have thought?"

Who'd have thought indeed? In fact, we know that gut health has a direct impact on mental health[92], but it's unusual for it to have such a massive effect.

WHY IS GUT HEALTH SO IMPORTANT?

The stomach and intestine (gastrointestinal tract or GIT) is the major portal through which we get all our nutrients and energy. If your gut isn't healthy, your body can't get what it needs to function properly. In addition, anything that affects the integrity of the GIT will also have an impact on how your body processes drugs.

The gut plays a crucial role in the normal running of the body. It breaks down the foods we eat. It allows the absorption of nutrients essential for everything from energy production to hormone balance to skin health to mental health to toxin and waste elimination. As if that wasn't enough, 70% of the immune system is based in the gut[93].

It doesn't take much to see that you should take good care of your digestive system if you want to enjoy good overall health.

THE MOST COMMON TYPES AND CAUSES OF GUT DISORDERS

Your gut may suffer from a wide range of issues, some of which may be symptomatic of a more serious problem. In many instances, gut issues will resolve themselves in time or by adjusting your diet.

It's important to be aware of what's normal and what's not as well as when you should be concerned. This is especially the case since many symptoms related to the gut have multiple potential causes.

Nausea and vomiting. Nausea and vomiting aren't diseases in their own right but rather a symptom of something else. The causes are wide ranging, including:

- Infection
- Food poisoning
- Motion sickness
- Overeating
- Blocked intestine
- Disease
- Concussion or brain injury
- Appendicitis
- Migraines

- Hangovers
- Drug side effects

If your nausea/vomiting has meant you haven't been able to eat for over 12 hours, or you've tried over the counter remedies and you still feel sick for over 24 hours, seek medical help. You should also consult a physician if your nausea/vomiting is accompanied by other symptoms. These include chest or abdominal pain, confusion, blurred vision, fever, stiff neck, fecal matter or smell in your vomit, or rectal bleeding.

Diarrhea. Diarrhea also has multiple causes. The most common is a virus, but it may also be a consequence of:

- Alcohol abuse
- Food allergies or intolerances
- Diabetes
- Intestinal diseases such as Crohn's disease or ulcerative colitis
- Bacteria
- Laxative abuse
- Medication side effects
- Hyperthyroidism
- Radiation therapy
- Cancer
- Surgery
- Malabsorption (problems absorbing certain nutrients).

Another bizarre cause of diarrhea is running. Some people get what's called 'runner's diarrhea' for reasons which haven't been determined. But that's still no excuse not to get some other form of exercise!

Seek medical advice if your diarrhea persists for more than two days or is accompanied with blood, excessive thirst, dry mouth, little or no urination, dark urine, weakness, dizziness, or severe pain.

Constipation. There are many potential explanations for why you may be constipated, although sometimes you may develop it for no discernible reason. These may be:

- Not eating enough fiber
- Not drinking enough fluids
- Not moving around or spending long periods sitting or lying down
- Not exercising
- Ignoring the urge to go to toilet
- Change in diet
- Side effect of medication
- Stress, anxiety, or depression
- Pregnancy or in the six weeks following birth

While constipation may also be caused by a medical condition, this is rare.

Consult a medical professional if your constipation is accompanied by pain or cramps and you can't pass gas. You should also seek help if it's a new problem and lifestyle changes aren't helping, if you have blood in your stool, you're losing weight for no reason, you have severe pain when you do manage to go to toilet, the size, shape, and consistently of your stool has changed, or your constipation has gone on for over two weeks.

Ulcers and heartburn. While these are two separate conditions, they frequently come hand in hand. An ulcer is a sore or hole which can occur in the lining of your stomach or intestine. Almost three quarters of people with an ulcer don't experience any symptoms[94].

If you're in the unlucky quarter that do, the most common symptom is a burning sensation in the upper abdomen. This may be accompanied by bloating, heartburn, and nausea.

Ulcers can usually be successfully treated and managed, but left untreated, they can become dangerous, leading to conditions such as stomach perforation, or gastrointestinal bleeding.

Heartburn may be caused by a number of factors, like certain foods, hiatal hernias or lifestyle risks such as smoking or being overweight. Ulcers are most frequently caused by a bacterium (Helicobacter pylori) or NSAIDs (Non-Steroidal Anti-Inflammatory Drugs).

Ulcers don't cause heartburn, but chronic reflux (GERD) can worsen or cause ulcers. One study found that 50% of people with GERD had ulcers[95]. Since the symptoms for heartburn and ulcers are similar, if you suspect a problem, consult a physician for an accurate diagnosis - **not** Dr.

Google! They will then be able to put together the most appropriate treatment plan. For example, if you're on NSAIDs, they'll be able to prescribe you alternative pain relief.

Irritable bowel syndrome (IBS). This is a common condition that affects the digestive system causing symptoms like cramps, bloating, diarrhea, and constipation. These can come and go, lasting from a few days to months. It is usually a lifelong problem, which can negatively impact a sufferer's quality of life. The exact cause is unknown, although there are theories that it could be down to food passing through the gut too quickly or slowly, oversensitive nerves in the gut, stress, or family history. Diet changes and medication may help manage the symptoms.

Celiac disease. Celiac disease is an autoimmune condition where the immune system has an abnormal reaction to gluten. This is a substance found in foods like bread, pasta, cereal, etc. You need to have eaten gluten in order to develop the condition, which results in the body's immune system producing antibodies to attack gluten. This makes the wall of the intestine red and inflamed. This damages the villi, meaning your body can't digest food effectively, bringing on symptoms of the disease.

It is unknown why people develop celiac disease. Family history plays a role, but environmental factors may also have a part. These include introducing gluten to a baby's diet too early, or infections like rotavirus in early childhood. There is only one treatment for celiac disease: stop eating gluten. It really is the case that food is your medicine if you're a celiac sufferer.

FOUR SIMPLE STEPS TO MAINTAIN GOOD GUT HEALTH

1. **Eat a balanced diet.** You probably don't need me to tell you what a balanced diet is. We all know we should eat plenty of fruit and vegetables, avoid processed foods, artificial sweeteners and added sugar. However, it can be difficult to eat healthily when ingredients are expensive and you don't have the time or energy to cook something after a long day at work.

   The benefits of eating healthily are well worth it and when you change your diet, you'll soon notice the change in your health. Start by making small changes, like having a salad for lunch or fruit for a snack. Many healthy meals can be made on a budget and you don't have to spend hours slaving over a hot stove to enjoy a tasty omelet or caesar salad.

2. **Observe good hygiene when cooking and eating.** As we discussed in the chapter on infection, proper hygiene is one of the most important steps in staying healthy. Wash your hands before preparing food and wash the food before preparing it. If you're lucky enough to have someone else cook for you, wash your hands before eating. And, of course, always wash your hands after going to the bathroom.

3. **Avoid overusing antibiotics.** We've already mentioned that antibiotic abuse has led to drug resistant bacteria. There's another reason why you should only take antibiotics when absolutely necessary - they can cause an imbalance in gut flora. Antibiotics affect bacteria indiscriminately, which means that they'll also wipe out the so-called 'good' bacteria which help keep your gut functioning properly.

4. **Take more probiotics (foods or supplements which contain microorganisms) and prebiotics (food for your microflora, generally high fiber).** This is especially important if you've been taking a course of antibiotics because it will help your gut flora repopulate faster. Pro- and prebiotics will help keep your gut healthy and balanced.

It's funny how medicine sometimes travels full circle. All those centuries ago, Hippocrates told us that food was the answer to good health. While modern medicine has given us ways of building upon what nature provides, we're increasingly realizing that the most important thing anyone can do to stay healthy is to eat a nutritious diet which supports the gut.

We're going to move even further down the body in the next chapter by taking a look at sexual health and how you can take care of yourself while enjoying a healthy sex life.

If this chapter on Gut Health has provoked a curiosity for more information on the topic, we encourage you to get a copy of our book **Plant Based Gut Health**. You'll find it on Amazon by searching for **LearnWell Books**

16

SEXUAL HEALTH & HEALTHY SEX

Keeping You In Business

What we used to do all night now takes us all night to do.

– Unknown

"How long have I been coming to this pharmacy, James?" Camille gave me an inquisitive look as I thought about her question. A well turned out woman in her late 40s, she'd been diagnosed with breast cancer a couple of years ago and had been coming to the pharmacy for the drugs which were part of her treatment.

"It's been a while," I replied. "Why?"

"I just want to be sure you can be discreet. I have a rather… delicate matter I need some advice on."

"You could be a brand new customer and your secret would still be safe with me," I promised her. "I'm the absolute soul of discretion. Trust me - I've seen it all."

"It's just that…" She sighed and bit her lip, building up the courage to say what was bothering her. I said nothing, giving her the space to talk. At last, she leaned forward, lowering her voice. "I keep getting these severe headaches whenever I have sex. They hit me whenever I… you know… climax. They're crushing, like something's pressing down at the top of my head. I don't get headaches any other time. It's become so bad, I just don't want to have sex anymore. I'm sure you can imagine how happy my husband is about that. I was hoping you could recommend something I could take for them. Regular painkillers don't seem to do anything."

"You could try these. They're a little stronger than most painkillers." I gave her a box of over-the-counter-meds. "But if I were you, I'd go back to your oncologist."

Camille paled. "You don't think I've got a brain tumor? I couldn't cope with that on top of breast cancer."

"No, no, nothing like that," I reassured her. "But there's a disorder known as benign sexual headache. It's rare and can only be diagnosed by ruling out other conditions. If that's what it is, then treatment is available and you can resume normal sexual relations without worrying about headaches."

Most of us are aware of the possibility of sexually transmitted infections such as chlamydia, syphilis, and HIV. We know that practising safe sex using a condom and limiting the number of partners we have will decrease our chances of contracting an STI. But in this chapter I want to focus on other sexual healh issues which are also common but have less awareness surrounding them.

TYPES OF SEXUAL DISORDERS

There are many different sexual disorders which may affect your ability to enjoy an active, healthy sex life. These include:

> **Low or high libido.** Your libido is your sex drive, which determines how frequently you do or don't want to have sex. It's natural to go through periods where your libido is lower or higher than normal for a range of reasons. When a couple have wildly differing libidos, it can cause problems in a relationship. If you feel your libido is an issue, it's best to consult your doctor in the first instance who can determine whether there is an underlying condition and advise you on appropriate treatments.
>
> **Erectile dysfunction.** Erectile dysfunction impacts approximately 30 million men in the US[96]. This is when you are unable to get or maintain a satisfactory erection for

intercourse. While it is more common among older men, it is not a normal part of the aging process, so you should speak to a medical professional if you are suffering from it. It may be a sign of a more serious underlying condition.

Pain or discomfort during sex. Both men and women can suffer from pain during or after sex. Women may feel it in their vagina or deeper in the pelvis, which can have a range of causes, including infection, menopause, lack of arousal, or an allergy. Men may experience it due to infection, a tight foreskin, miniscule tears in the foreskin, inflammation of the prostate gland, or testicular swelling. If you are finding sex uncomfortable, you should seek medical help to rule out a serious underlying problem.

Priapism. This is a long-lasting, painful erection. It can cause permanent damage if left untreated.

Hypogonadism. This is when your sex glands (gonads) produce little or no sex hormones. These are the testes in men and the ovaries in women.

Symptoms in women can include:

- A lack of menstruation
- Slow or no breast growth
- Hot flashes
- Loss of body hair
- Low libido
- A milky discharge from the breasts

Male symptoms may include:

- A loss of body hair
- Loss of muscle
- Abnormal breast growth
- Reduced growth of penis and testicles
- Erectile dysfunction
- Osteoporosis
- Low libido
- Infertility
- Fatigue
- Hot flashes

Since hypogonadism responds well to treatment, you should consult a medical professional if you notice any of these symptoms.

THE CAUSES OF SEXUAL DISORDERS

While some may assume that STIs are the main cause of a sexual disorder, in fact there are many reasons why your sexual health may be suffering. These may include:

- Medical conditions such as diabetes, or cancer
- Obesity
- Hormonal imbalances
- The menopause

- Medications such as metoclopramide (an anti-sickness medication), methyldopa (prescribed for high blood pressure), antipsychotics, etc.

- Endometriosis

Since sexual disorders are frequently a sign of a more serious underlying condition, you should always go and get yourself checked out by a medical professional if you've noticed something's wrong. Much as it might feel embarrassing to talk about something so private, trust me. We've seen it all. Nothing embarrasses us!

COMMON TREATMENTS FOR SEXUAL DISORDERS

Since there are so many sexual disorders, it would be impossible to dig deeply into all the different treatments, especially since they very much depend on the problem and its cause. However, I wanted to give you a brief overview of some of the more common treatments so you know what to expect and what questions to ask if you need any of them.

> **Sildenafil.** You probably know this under the brand name Viagra, although it's also sold as Aronix, Liberize, Nipatra, Revatio, and Grandipam. This is commonly used to treat erectile dysfunction. Some claim that it can have a similar stimulating effect on women, but the evidence for this is unclear. It is taken orally or by injection and the effects come on within 20 minutes, lasting for roughly two hours. An alternative is tadalafil (Cialis). This is taken in pill form, with onset occurring after half an hour and the effect lasting up to 36 hours. Like all drugs, they come with side

effects, the most common being headaches, heartburn and flushed skin. If you have cardiovascular disease, you shouldn't take sildenafil or tadalafil without first consulting a physician to make sure it's suitable for you. It should also be avoided if you're taking nitrates because it may cause a major drop in blood pressure. In rare cases, it can cause priapism, vision problems and loss of hearing. Do not take sildenafil within four hours of taking an alpha blocker.

Alprostadil. This medication makes the blood vessels expand, helping you have an erection. It is either injected directly into the penis or can be used as a suppository placed into the opening at the tip of the penis. It should only be used if you are suffering from erectile dysfunction, since it can cause permanent damage if not used properly. It starts to work after 5-20 minutes and then you need to wait 10-30 minutes before having sex. The erection should last for about an hour and may remain after ejaculation. Do not use alprostadil more than three times a week, leaving at least 24 hours between uses.

Alprostadil is not suitable for everyone. Tell your doctor if:

- You've ever had an allergic reaction to it or any other substances
- If you're taking any other medications, including herbal or dietary supplements
- If you have a penile implant
- If you have a history of priapism
- If you have any birth defects with your penis

- If you suffer from bleeding problems or conditions which cause slower blood flow
- If you're taking blood thinners
- If you have a penile infection
- If your penis is red or itchy
- If you have Peyronie's disease.

Vacuum erectile device (VED). This is another treatment for erectile dysfunction. It involves placing a tube over the penis, using a pump to pull air out of the tube to create a vacuum, which will cause an erection. Once the penis is erect, you place a band over the base of the penis to maintain the erection. This band should not be left on for longer than 30 minutes or it may cause damage. Side effects may include a cold penis while the band is in place. You can counteract this with a warm complex. You may also find it hard to ejaculate because the band stops semen from coming through. (Note that this is unsuitable as a form of contraceptive.) You may see small red spots below the skin or mild bruising. If this is the case, stop using the device until these have cleared up. VEDs are generally safe, but you should check with your doctor before using one if you have a bleeding disorder, are taking blood thinning medications, or have a condition which may cause priapism.

Lubricants. If you are suffering from vaginal dryness, lubricants and moisturizers may help. Lubricants are used when you have sex. Most can be bought over the counter, although some are also available on prescription. They can be water-based, silicone-based, or oil-based. Note that oil-based products may damage the latex in condoms, so use with caution if you want to avoid pregnancy or STIs. Which type you use is very much a case of personal preference, so it's worth experimenting with the different types to see which ones you prefer. Vaginal moisturizers help retain moisture in the vagina. You can apply these on a regular basis and at least 2 hours before intercourse.

PREVENTING SEXUAL DISORDERS

As with any health issue, prevention is much better than the cure. There are many things you can do to lower your chances of suffering from a sexual disorder:

Diet. You've heard me mention it before, but a nutritious, balanced diet is so important when it comes to your general health and wellbeing and this includes your sexual health. A good diet helps prevent conditions such as diabetes which are a risk factor for sexual dysfunction. Some people swear by natural aphrodisiacs such as chocolate, oysters, and spicy food, but the evidence for their effectiveness is scant[97]. It's more likely that the romantic environment of a nice meal in a restaurant creates an arousing effect than the food! There's nothing wrong with experimenting with food to see if you notice any impact on your libido, but you should be aware that some supplements come with potentially severe side effects. For example, Spanish fly, commonly advertised as a natural aphrodisiac, can cause kidney damage and bleeding. Other supplements have been found to include prescription drug ingredients without it being listed on the label, which could be dangerous when taken with other drugs or if you have certain medical conditions.

Weight loss. Obesity has been proven to have a connection with many sexual disorders. For example, abdominal obesity has been shown to increase the chances of erectile dysfunction, especially in older men. A BMI of 28 can increase a man's risk of erectile dysfunction by an incredible 90%. What's more, it can also increase your chances of infertility. Studies have shown that for every 3 point increase in BMI, a couple was 10% more likely to be infertile. Fortunately, these effects can be reversed with weight loss[98].

Exercise. Regular exercise helps keep you in top shape and this includes in the bedroom. A University of California study found that men who exercised regularly had more sex, more reliable erections and more satisfying orgasms[99]. Women also benefit from exercise. According to a study by the University of Texas, women who exercised experienced greater arousal, which led to better sex[100]. So if you needed an excuse to hit the gym, maybe this is it!

CONTRACEPTION

Contraception can be a controversial topic for some. Ultimately it is up to the individual to decide whether they want to use contraception and why. No form of contraception is 100% effective (with the exception of sterilization), but used properly, it can help avoid unwanted pregnancy and limit the risk of contracting an STI. Some hormonal contraceptives may be taken to tackle hormonal problems rather than for contraceptive purposes per se.

The main forms of contraception are:

Condoms. (Male and female.) Condoms are the only form of contraceptive which also offer protection from STIs. Male condoms are a sheath which fits over the penis. Female condoms are worn inside the vagina. They form a barrier between the sperm and egg, preventing pregnancy. They are 98% effective when used properly, but they can slip off or break during sex[101]. If this happens, you may need emergency contraceptive and may want to get yourself tested for STIs. Condoms have a use by date which you should adhere to. Do not reuse condoms, especially since you may be able to get them for free from family planning clinics, so there's no excuse to try to save money. Some people find condoms uncomfortable or that stopping to put one on interrupts the mood.

Intrauterine device (IUD) or intrauterine system (IUS). These are small T-shaped devices placed into the womb by a medical professional. Once in place, they release copper or hormones which help prevent pregnancy. Properly fitted, they are over 99% effective[102] and last for up to 10 years. They work straight away. They do not interfere with breastfeeding or any medications you may be taking. If you decide you would like to try for a baby, you can get pregnant as soon as the device is removed. (Note that if you don't want to get pregnant and you're having your IUD/IUS removed, you should use a condom for 7 days beforehand.) Some women find that their periods become heavier or more painful with an IUD. If you get an infection when you have one fitted, this may develop into a pelvic infection if left untreated. Since they do not protect against STIs, you may need to use condoms as well if you're not in a monogamous relationship. Some women report that having one fitted is incredibly painful, so be prepared to be kind to yourself immediately afterwards and stock up on painkillers.

Birth control pills. Birth control pills deliver a daily dose of hormones to prevent pregnancy. They can also help with other hormonal issues. There are two different types - combination pills which have estrogen and progestin and progestin-only pills. It is a highly effective form of contraceptive. The main reasons it fails are usually because someone forgets to take a pill, loses their pills or doesn't refill their prescription on time. While the pill should be 99% effective, when not taken properly, this can drop down to 91%[103]. The pill is generally safe, but when you start taking it, you may experience headaches, nausea, sore breasts, spotting, or changes in your period. These side effects usually go away after a couple of months, but if not, ask your doctor if you can try a different type. For some women, the side effects of the pill are useful. They can help reduce cramps and premenstrual syndrome and make your period lighter and more regular. You can even use the pill to miss a period. Be aware that some medications, e.g. those used to treat epilepsy, can interfere with the effectiveness of the pill. Tell your doctor if you are taking any other drugs, including natural supplements or over-the-counter medications.

Implants. The contraceptive implant is a small plastic rod placed under the skin in your upper arm by a trained medical professional. It releases progestogen into your bloodstream to stop pregnancy for up to three years and is over 99% effective[104]. It is particularly suitable for women who can't use contraception containing estrogen or struggle to remember to take a pill regularly. It can be taken out at any time and your fertility will return soon after. It may not be right for you if you:

Think you're pregnant

- Don't want your periods to change
- Are taking other medications which will affect the implant
- Have unexplained bleeding between periods or following sex
- Have arterial disease
- Have a history of heart disease or stroke
- Have liver disease
- Have breast cancer or are in remission from breast cancer

Since implants don't protect against STIs, you may need to use condoms as well while you have one fitted.

Sterilization. If you have decided that your family is complete and you don't want any more children, a more permanent form of contraception is sterilization. This is a medical method designed to leave you unable to reproduce. There are a number of types of sterilization, but the most common are tubal ligation (women) and vasectomy (men). If you subsequently change your mind, it may be possible to reverse the sterilization, but this cannot be relied upon, particularly if it's been a long time since the surgery. If you have had a hysterectomy (removal of the uterus), this cannot be reversed. Like any surgeries, sterilization comes with a certain level of risk, with a higher risk associated with tubal ligations than vasectomies. Tubal ligations may cause bleeding inside the abdomen, infection, damage to other organs in the abdomen, or ectopic pregnancy. Vasectomies may cause chronic pain, bleeding, bruising, and infection. It is also possible to fall pregnant following sterilization, particularly in the first few months, so you may want to use another form of contraception in the meantime.

Sexual health is such a vast subject, I could write an entire book about it. Hopefully, the brief outline provided here will have given you an idea of what's normal and what's not. Remember - if you have any concerns, don't be afraid to consult a trusted medical professional. We're here to set your mind at ease and make sure sexual disorders don't stop you from enjoying a healthy sex life.

In the next chapter, we'll be delving into the difficult subject of cancer, a condition which struck Camille and many of my other customers. Most of us will know someone who has been affected by cancer at some point during our lives, so it's important we're all aware of what to look out for. Early intervention is crucial for long-term prognosis.

17

CANCER

Dodge It Or Increase Your Chances Of Beating It

I'm going to beat this cancer or die trying.

– Michael Landon

"How are you doing, Amanda?" I smiled to welcome one of my favorite customers into the pharmacy. Amanda had been diagnosed with ovarian cancer a few years ago and she'd shared stories of her battle against the disease until she'd gone into remission. However, six months after she'd been given the all clear, she'd been showing signs of the cancer returning. A PET/CT scan had shown a recurrence in the pelvis. She'd had surgery to remove the mass followed by chemotherapy and had gone into remission again.

"Fine." Amanda's returning smile was weak, barely there.

"Are you sure?" I raised an eyebrow.

She sighed. "I think the cancer's back again. I'm scheduled for another scan next week. I don't know what I'm going to do if the results come back positive."

"I'm so sorry to hear that. You know that I'm always here for you if you need someone to talk to."

Amanda's scans showed that the cancer had returned, another mass growing in her pelvis near to the previous lump. My heart broke for her when she told me. She had two young children and the thought of them being without their mother was awful.

"I'm scheduled for surgery next week," Amanda said. "They said they want to get it out as soon as possible, just in case. My mom's looking after the children so Mike can support me. We haven't told them what's going on. I couldn't bear to see the look on their faces if they thought I was going to die."

"I'm sure everything's going to be fine," I reassured her. "Can I offer you a little advice?"

"Of course. You know I'm always interested in what you've got to say, James."

"If I were you, I would get them to get the tumor examined for drug resistance. The fact that you're getting recurrent tumors in such a localized area tells me there's something else going on."

"I'll do that. Thanks!"

A few months later, Amanda was back in my pharmacy looking healthier than I'd ever seen her.

"Sorry it's been so long since I've been in, but we've just come back from Disneyland."

"Everything's going well then?"

"Yes, Mike wanted us to celebrate as a family because it looks like we've solved the riddle of why the tumors kept coming back. They discovered that the tumor cells had developed a resistance to the type of chemotherapy I was on. They've switched up my drugs and it's looking good. Obviously, it's still too early to tell, but the doctors are hopeful that this time I'll be in remission for good."

The doctors were right. Changing Amanda's treatment finally tackled the root problem and to this day, Amanda remains cancer free.

Cancer

Cancer is one of the leading causes of death worldwide. Approximately 39.5% of us will be diagnosed with cancer at some point during our lives[105]. With advances in medical care and improved living conditions, the survival rate is increasing, but it very much depends on the type of cancer and how early it's detected. This is why it's so important to be aware of the signs so you can get a diagnosis as soon as possible. Treatments will vary depending on your individual circumstances, so it's best to get yourself referred to a specialist who will be able to put together an appropriate plan for your specific type of cancer.

WHAT IS CANCER?

Cancer is a disease in which some of your body cells start to grow uncontrollably, spreading to other parts of the body. Cancer can originate almost anywhere in the human body, although the most common types are breast, prostate, lung, and colorectal[106].

There are three stages to the development of cancer:

>**Initiation.** This is when the specific parts of the genes controlling cell division mutate, preventing the body from killing abnormal cells. There are many different reasons why this might happen, such as exposure to radiation, chemicals, and toxins. Not all mutations will lead to cancer. Most of the time, the body will naturally correct a mutation. Cancer tends to develop when there have been multiple mutations.
>
>**Promotion.** In this stage, the body provides an ideal environment to promote the replication of abnormal cells.

Some food substances or additives can encourage the growth of cancerous cells. For example, processed meat is known to have an increased risk of causing cancer, as is alcohol[107].

Progression. This is when cells become malignant and develop into full-blown cancer. Cancer cells can invade other parts of the body, ignoring the body's natural signals which regulate cell growth and division.

There are many different types of cancer:

Carcinomas are cancers that start in the skin or the tissues lining other organs.

Sarcoma is a cancer of connective tissues like bones, muscles, cartilage, and blood vessels.

Leukemia is a cancer of the bone marrow.

Lymphoma and myeloma are cancers of the immune system.

You may also have cancer in any of your organs, such as lung, liver, brain, etc. or in other body parts, such as the throat or mouth.

INCREASING YOUR RISK OF CANCER

While we do not always know what causes cancer, we do know that there are a number of factors which increase your chances of developing this devastating disease:

Lifestyle. The connection between smoking and lung (and other types of) cancer has been known since at least the 1940s[108]. Where once it was recommended as a healthy activity, we now know that smoking carries with it a number of risks to health and very little benefit. Likewise, alcohol is associated with at least seven types of cancer[109]. A sedentary lifestyle might also increase your chances of cancer. Scientists are unsure why, although it is believed that poor circulation and higher levels of insulin in the blood may be a factor[110].

Diet. Here it is again - one of the simplest ways to care for your health. Eating a diet high in preservatives, food additives, sugar, and calories increases your chances of cancer[111]. So, if this book has helped you identify that there may be some room for improvement in your diet, this may be the incentive you need to make the change. Remember - even small adjustments can make a big difference. You don't have to radically change the way you eat overnight. In fact, it could be a major shock to the system if you do, bringing on a healing crisis[112]. But gradually reducing the things you know negatively impact your health and replacing them with healthy alternatives will reduce your risk of cancer very quickly.

Location. Where you live can increase your chances of developing cancer due to environmental factors. Rural areas are generally safer than urban ones[113].

Gender. Different types of cancer are more likely to affect the different genders. For example, while men can suffer from breast cancer, it is rare, whereas it's one of the most common cancers in women. The different anatomies of men and women also mean that there are gender specific cancers, such as prostate, ovarian, and cervical.

THE SEVEN WARNING SIGNS OF CANCER

Different cancers come with different symptoms. Some can be symptomless until they are highly advanced. For example, ovarian cancer has been dubbed "The Silent Killer" because it is very difficult to detect. Any unusual or persistent symptoms should be checked out by a medical professional to rule out any problems.

The most common warning signs are:

- Extreme changes in bowel habits, blood in your urine or stools, difficulties going to the toilet, etc.
- Sores which don't heal.
- A lump in the breast (even small ones).
- Sudden changes in the appearance of moles.
- Unusual bleeding.
- A disturbing or persistent cough or hoarseness.
- Indigestion or problems swallowing.

In addition, you may want to get your child checked out if they experience sudden unexplained weight loss, you notice a whitish spot in their pupils, they have recurrent fevers, unexplained bruises, or pains which don't have a discernible cause.

If you notice any of these signs, go to your doctor and ask to be screened. These symptoms may also be the result of other conditions, so do not automatically assume you have cancer. Going to the doctor will allow you to know exactly what's going on so you can make an informed choice about your next steps.

HOW TO LOWER YOUR RISK OF GETTING CANCER AND GET THE BEST OUT OF YOUR CANCER MEDS

Limiting your exposure to those factors which are known carcinogens will help reduce your chances of developing cancer. If you have been diagnosed with cancer, making certain changes will also help your treatment be more effective. While it may feel like you're helpless in the face of this terrible disease, taking action to improve your health can support you to feel more in control, giving you a more positive mindset for the challenges ahead.

> **Lifestyle changes.** Just as your lifestyle can increase your chances of getting cancer, it can also lower your chances. Eat a diet with plenty of fiber and low in fatty, processed foods and red meats. Get regular physical exercise. Stop smoking and reduce your alcohol intake.
>
> **Take supplements.** We'll be looking at supplements in greater detail later in this book, but some of the supplements which may help fight cancer or combat the side effects of your treatment include:
>
> - Vitamin D
> - Omega-3 fatty acids
> - Probiotics

FOR EXCELLENT HEALTH DO THIS

- Calcium
- Folic acid
- Vitamin B6[114].

Note that supplements are not a replacement for cancer treatment and there is no scientific evidence that any supplement can prevent, control, or cure cancer on its own.

Get regular medical check ups. You can be screened for cancer once or twice a year. This may be particularly important if you have a family history of cancer.

Get yourself genetically tested. It is known that some genes increase your risk of cancer, such as BRCA1 and BRCA2[115]. You may want to consider getting yourself genetically tested to see if you carry any of these genes to take a proactive approach to cancer. Before undergoing any tests, consider what difference a positive result would make to you and whether it would be more reassuring to know or not.

Follow professional advice about your drugs. You should always take your drugs as prescribed, but it is particularly important when it comes to cancer treatment. Ask your doctor about side effects to be aware of, as well as how to take your drugs and for how long. You may want to set reminders to tell you to take your medication, since brain fog is a common side effect of cancer treatment[116].

Survival rates from cancer are increasing all the time as we become aware of what to look for and develop more effective treatments[117]. If you receive a diagnosis, you have a good chance of beating the disease, particularly if you catch the cancer early. Making the changes recommended in this chapter will help increase your chances of fighting this deadly condition so you can join the ranks of the ever-increasing numbers of survivors and live to a ripe old age.

Speaking of old age, in the next chapter we'll be looking at the specific health requirements of the elderly. You'll learn all about the paradox of medicating the elderly and what you can do to get the most out of your medications.

18

MEDICAL CARE OVER 65

Managing Pills. Avoiding Spills

The best tunes are played on the oldest fiddles!

– Ralph Waldo Emerson

I handed over a large bag filled with various drugs to an old man who'd come in for his regular prescriptions.

"Here you go, Mr. Jonas. That should keep you going for a while."

"Yeah, right." The man shook his head as he took the bag. "I'll be back before you know it. I've got to take one drug for my arthritis, another to counteract the side effects of that drug, another for the side effects of *that* drug, and I've forgotten most of the reasons why I'm on the others. I don't know. It seems to me that it shouldn't be this difficult to stay alive!"

"I hear you." I smiled at him in reassurance. "Still, it's better than the alternative…"

"I guess," said Mr. Jonas. "I suppose I should count my blessings I'm able to afford all my medications. A friend of my wife wound up in hospital because she couldn't pay for her prescriptions, so she was only taking half a dose of her heart pills. I must admit there's been times when I've been tempted to cut back on my drugs. It's no fun when you have to swallow a handful of horse pills with every meal!"

While you may be feeling young at heart, if you're over 65, you're considered old for clinical purposes. There is a paradox when it comes to treating the elderly. Older people have more health conditions and may require more medications. However, they are also more sensitive to drugs, so are more likely to have adverse reactions, meaning they need fewer meds. When dealing with an elderly patient, a healthcare provider always has to consider the fine balance between more and less medications.

Just as children process drugs differently to adults, elderly people also find that their bodies have changed. The absorption, distribution, metabolism, and excretion of drugs is different to when they were younger. This may be due to impairments in their kidneys, liver, stomach, etc. or may simply be because they're more sensitive to medications now.

Many elderly people find themselves needing to take multiple medications to treat different concurrent medical issues. For example, it's not unknown for someone to have diabetes, hypertension, arthritis, and heart problems at the same time. They all require multiple medications to control the condition. Then you have the problem of whether these medications will interact negatively with concurrent conditions or each other.

The risk of hospitalization because of negative reactions to medications is almost 6 times higher for the elderly than the rest of the population. Research has shown that over 55% of elderly patients do not take their medications properly. With up to 30% of hospital readmissions due to taking medications incorrectly, this is a serious issue[118].

The main reasons why the elderly don't take their medications properly include:

> **Not remembering how they were supposed to take their drugs.** Even when given written and verbal information, many struggle to recall what they're supposed to do with their drugs.
>
> **Forgetting to take their drugs.**

Forgetting whether they've taken their drugs. Even when someone has taken a pill, half an hour later they may struggle to remember whether they really did take it, so take another just in case.

Not knowing why they need to take a certain drug. There may be some confusion or uncertainty over the purpose of a particular medication. As such, someone may stop taking it because they don't like the way it makes them feel or they feel better so don't think they need it anymore. This is problematic because the medication may be an essential part of their treatment.

Too many drugs to take. Seniors may have to take multiple medications at a time and do not like taking so many pills or forget how to take each one.

Struggling to physically take their medication. There may be a physical reason why someone can't take medication, such as arthritis, visual impairments, or cognitive impairments. They may not have the support of a caregiver to help them take their medications.

Can't afford them. Some seniors may struggle to meet the cost of all their medications, so spread out their pills or take half doses so they last longer.

Fear. Many seniors get health information online. They may research potential side effects and become afraid to take their medications.

Distrust. Some seniors are suspicious of their health care providers because of concerns over their motives or those of other members in the healthcare system, particularly the pharmaceutical companies.

All of these are common issues which, unfortunately, can make health problems worse when a treatment regime isn't properly followed. If you are aware that you are likely to be affected by these, or you have an elderly friend or relative you are concerned about, put into place some action steps to minimize the risk of improper use of prescription drugs.

HOW THE ELDERLY CAN GET THE BEST OUT OF THEIR MEDICATIONS

1. **Keep detailed records of your medications**

    Of all the material in your Workbook, the content related to this chapter is arguably the most critical. It's particularly important if you're elderly and taking a lot of different medications. The charts we've provided will make it easy for you and your healthcare team to keep a track of medications and their side effects. It will help you replace medications which are inappropriate and add details of how to take important medications.

    You should always make note of all the drugs you've taken within the last six months. Include directions of how to take each one and note the generic name rather than the brand name so you know exactly how much you should be taking. So, for example, note down "Losartan 50mg once daily" rather than "Cozavan once daily." You can find the generic name on the drug packaging. Alternatively, your pharmacist will be happy to help. Also record any over-the-counter drugs or supplements you're taking or have taken within the past week.

2. **Keep detailed records of all your medical conditions**

    This should include a history of any serious diseases you've experienced in your lifetime, as well as allergies, adverse drug reactions and any chronic, or life threatening diseases your close relatives have had. You should also make note of any treatable disease you've developed over the past 3-6 months or are currently suffering from.

3. **Keep detailed records of any lifestyle habits which may be an influence**

    Make note of any habits and their frequency, e.g. smoking, alcohol use, recreational drug taking, etc. If you've stopped any of these habits, write down when you stopped.

4. **Ask your pharmacist for help**

    If you think you'll struggle to keep your own Workbook, ask your local pharmacy if they offer this as a service. Many do and are more than willing to support you to stay healthy with your medications. You can also ask your healthcare team for a copy of your medical records if you need to remind yourself of your medical history.

5. **Try to stay consistent with your healthcare team**

    Wherever possible, try to use the same healthcare professionals for your treatment. You might like to have a regular family doctor, nurse, and pharmacist. The fewer medical professionals you see, the easier it is to maintain accurate records. There's also a lot to be said for developing personal relationships so that your healthcare team knows your usual state of health and can identify any changes more easily.

6. **Put a strategy in place to remind you to take your medications**

   There are a number of things you can do to remember to take your medications. I recommend using a combination of pill boxes, calendars and mobile apps, but get creative. Whatever works best for you is the right strategy.

   Pill boxes have compartments for different days of the week so you know what you're supposed to take and when. These can be refilled once a week, which makes staying on schedule simpler. However, don't put nitroglycerin or any volatile pills in pill boxes. They can evaporate and lose their potency if not stored correctly[119].

If you have a caregiver, get them actively involved in your medication regime. You could set a reminder on your phone to remind you to take your meds and then make a record that you've actually taken them so you don't have to worry about overdosing. You'll find we've created these simple tools for your use in your Workbook.

For more inspiration, you might like to talk about your regime in the LearnWell Community.

If you look after yourself, there's no reason why you can't enjoy a long and healthy life. Your healthcare team has your best interests at heart and will only prescribe you medications which are genuinely necessary. Staying on top of your medication regimen will help you maintain good health for a long time to come.

We've mentioned supplements in many chapters in this book. It's now time to look at this subject in more depth so you know what supplements you should and shouldn't take to support your health.

19

SUPPLEMENTS
A Vital Part Of Your Vitality

Getting all of the nutrients you need simply cannot be done without supplements.

– Steven Gundry

As a pharmacist, I get plenty of customers coming in asking about what supplements they should be taking. It's a tricky question to answer. Personally, I take a high quality multivitamin and if I feel myself coming down with a cold, I'm a big fan of drinking honey and lemon in hot water. But that doesn't mean that everyone needs supplements nor that all supplements are created equal.

There is a lot of noise and potential conflicts of interest when it comes to supplements. The regulation on supplements is pretty lax when compared to medicines, which means you can't know what you're getting with the same amount of confidence. That's not to say that there aren't beneficial supplements, which is why this chapter is going to guide you through the maze of available supplements.

DO I NEED SUPPLEMENTS?

The short answer is: it depends. A healthy person eating a balanced diet which provides adequate nutrition probably doesn't need to take any supplements. However, there are individuals who may benefit from taking some supplements. These include:

- People on restricted diets. This may be out of choice (e.g. vegans) or due to medical conditions (e.g. celiac disease).

- Pregnant women may need to take magnesium to help prevent preeclampsia, folic acid to protect against birth defects, calcium, omega-3, etc.

- Babies who are being weaned from formula. Fortified milk may help. Seek the support of a nutritionist who specializes in babies.

- People with nutritional deficiencies.

- People who are suffering from disease, whether chronic conditions such as cystic fibrosis or Crohn's disease, or acute illnesses such as flu, COVID, or the common cold. Be aware that some supplements can combat the side effects of meds while others are supposed to improve the effectiveness of meds or even the symptoms of the disease itself.

- People taking certain medications.

Always consult your healthcare team before taking any supplements. This is because supplements may interfere with your medication regime. Some may be toxic in large quantities, such as vitamin D, which can harm your kidneys, or calcium, which can settle in the arteries[120].

HELPFUL SUPPLEMENTS

Supplements should not be used as an attempt to cure a disease. Most supplements are only tested for their safety with scant evidence available for their efficacy. Any claims made about a supplement are unlikely to be backed by the FDA.

However, there are some exceptions, such as the use of vitamin K to prevent blood clots. Some situations where supplements may help include:

Hormonal imbalances. Supplements such as ashwaganda[121] and evening primrose[122] may help with problems associated with hormonal imbalances such as irregular periods or menopause symptoms.

Sleep issues. Melatonin[123] may be used to address sleep problems.

Sexual dysfunction. Many people turn to supplements to help with sexual problems rather than seek professional medical help. Yohimbe[124] and Spanish fly[125] are most commonly taken, although the evidence is unclear as to their efficacy.

Common cold. Vitamins C, and D as well as zinc and echinacea are all proven to have a positive effect on the symptoms of a cold[126].

Stress. Ginseng[127] may be a good idea if you are suffering from the symptoms of stress.

Mental health. Omega-3[128] and St. John's Wort[129] are both proven to have a positive impact on the symptoms of depression with potentially fewer side effects than traditional antidepressants. However, they should be handled with caution because St. John's Wort in particular can interfere with the effectiveness of other drugs.

Irritable bowel syndrome. Psyllium husk[130] has been shown to relieve the symptoms associated with irritable bowel syndrome.

Liver disease. Milk thistle[131] has been shown to reduce the death rate associated with liver disease, making it an excellent supplement to take if you have any liver problems.

While many of these supplements have positive effects, anything which can heal can also harm. Just as with traditional medicines, they may cause adverse effects and can interact with any prescription drugs to make them less effective. You should always inform your doctor and pharmacist if you're taking any supplements before taking prescription drugs.

HOW TO TAKE SUPPLEMENTS PROPERLY

- Research the dosage and never be tempted to take more than the recommended amount. You can overdose on a supplement, which may be toxic in large doses. You might like to do a search for scientific studies about a supplement to see whether it does what is claimed.

- Never use any supplement without the guidance of a pharmacist. We can advise you on the best way to take them.

- If you react badly to any supplement, stop taking it immediately and tell your healthcare provider. If you're keeping your Workbook, you should also update it with this information.

- Just to reiterate, always tell your doctor or pharmacist if you are taking any supplements or are planning to start. They will be able to advise you if it is safe and suitable and adjust your medication regime if necessary.

20

HOW TO G.R.O.W. UP HEALTHY

Your Action Plan
For Optimal Health

I believe that the greatest gift you can give your family and the world is a healthy you.

– Joyce Meyer

We've covered a huge amount of material in this book. I've structured it so you can always return to a relevant chapter at any time to refresh your memory and remind yourself about the best approach to that particular area of health.

Now we're going to pull it all together and apply all the knowledge you've learned to set your personal health goals and create an action plan to achieve them.

YOU HAVE TO SET SMART GOALS IF YOU WANT TO GROW

Your action plan will allow you to GROW:

> **G - Goals** must be SMART. This means they are specific, measurable, attainable, relevant (to your ambitions), and time-bound. It's important to set goals for yourself if you want to enjoy optimal health. It's not enough to say "I want to be fit and healthy." What does that look like for you? Does it mean eating nutritious food at every meal? Having three regular meals a day? Being able to run up and down the stairs without getting out of breath? Are your goals within your abilities? If, for example, you suffer from rheumatoid arthritis, you might want to have modest physical goals which keep you mobile and flexible but don't push your body too far. Putting a time limit on your goals enables you to track your progress and look back over what you've achieved to see if you should be doing things any differently.

R - Reality. Take an honest look at your current reality. If you suffer from any health conditions, you might want to discuss your proposed goals with your healthcare team to make sure they're realistic. If you want to start running marathons but the furthest you've ever run is down to the bus stop, you might want to work on shorter distances first. I recommend people carry out a SWOT analysis, which involves looking at your Strengths and Weaknesses, as well as potential Opportunities and Threats so you can play to your strengths while working on your weaknesses. Also consider what might get in the way of you achieving your goals so you can put plans in place for overcoming any obstacles.

O - Opportunity. Consider what your available opportunities are when it comes to your health. Maybe you want to cut back on the number of meds you take. You could discuss alternatives with your doctor, consider whether any of your conditions might be managed with a change in diet or lifestyle, look into whether there are any new treatments or approaches which you could try. There might be support groups for your condition, either locally or online, which can give you ideas of different approaches. Perhaps your opportunities exist around weight loss or even healthy weight gains. Maybe your biggest goal is to quit smoking. Survey all your opportunities and choose those that are the most attainable whilst delivering the biggest benefit to you.

W - Will. This is all about how determined you are to achieve your goals. Look at the opportunities you've identified and decide to focus on one or two to begin with as you work towards your goals. Examine your list of strengths and consider which ones will help you in the process. Consider the most likely weaknesses and threats which will get in your way and how you can minimize them. In this instance, threats aren't medical conditions but anything in yourself or your environment which may hinder you from GROWing to achieve your goals.

Now that you have your goal(s), it's time to record them and build a simple plan to achieve them. In your Workbook you'll find space to do that with helpful guiding prompts.

FIRST STEPS TO TAKING CHARGE OF YOUR OWN HEALTH

1. After you've finished reading this book, go back and re-read the chapters which are applicable to you. Make notes on how the information provided can support your goals.

2. Complete your Workbook following the outline in Chapter 20.

3. If you haven't already, pick your healthcare team. If possible, it's best to work with the same health professionals over a long time. Too many cooks spoil the broth - one family doctor, pharmacist and potentially a nurse are more than enough for a solid team. Consider how you're going to develop positive relationships with these professionals.

4. Set aside time every week to learn more about your meds or those your relatives are taking.

5. Always keep your Workbook with you when you go for a medical checkup or visit the doctor.

6. Come up with a strategy for having your Workbook accessible to healthcare professionals in the event of an emergency.

    a. It is a good idea to list your family doctor among your emergency contacts.

    b. You might like to make a copy of your Workbook and give that to your carer or emergency contact.

HEALTH GOAL-SETTING, AN EXAMPLE

There's no right or wrong way to write an action plan. There's just what works for you. Everyone's goals are different depending on their personal circumstances.

For the purposes of this exercise, we're going to work on the goal of creating your Workbook.

G - GOAL

This is a SMART goal:

- It's specific (you know exactly what you're going to do)
- It's measurable (either you've written your Journal by the end of the week or not)
- It's achievable (you should be able to create a Journal in one week)
- It's relevant (having a Workbook supports any other health goals)

- It's time dependent (you'll know if you've done your Journal or not by the end of the week).

R - REALITY

Do you have access to all the information you'll need? For example, your health records? Can you list out your allergies or chronic medical conditions?

- Assess your strengths and weaknesses.

    Strengths - what personal attributes do you have which will help you put together your Journal within your stipulated time frame? E.g. access to a pharmacy, computer literacy, support from a friend or loved one, etc.

    Weaknesses - what personal attributes are getting in the way of you creating your Workbook? E.g. lack of knowledge, no relationship with a helpful doctor or pharmacist, lack of understanding about the Journal format, etc.

O - OPPORTUNITIES

Think about the opportunities available to you to help you write your Journal.

- Are there any pharmacies nearby? Can you ask a pharmacist to help you with your Journal?
- Can you ask a pharmacist or doctor to educate you about your medications/conditions?

- Do you have good access to the internet? Can you look online for materials to help you with your Journal?

Also consider any threats/external factors which may prevent you writing your Journal so you can think of ways of overcoming them.

- If the pharmacist or doctor is too busy to help right now, can you schedule a later appointment with them?
- If you have a busy week ahead of you, can you get someone else to help out so you can make the time for your Journal?

W - WILL

How are you going to make sure you follow through on your commitment to completing your Workbook? How can you make the most of your opportunities and how serious are you about moving past any threats? Do you have any friends or relatives who can support you to make sure you create your Journal within the week?

Your Workbook is the first step of taking control of your health. That's why I've used it as an example goal in this section and why the final chapter is dedicated solely to this subject.

This book has taken you through everything you need to know to take control of your health and get the most out of your medical team. Follow the advice in this book and you'll receive a truly personalized approach which takes into account your specific needs.

Please make the most of the Workbook we've provided for you. This is an invaluable document which you can present to every

FOR EXCELLENT HEALTH DO THIS

healthcare professional to give them a full picture of your health history and current status. This will save time explaining every little detail as well as allow them to observe details you may otherwise forget to mention.

Establish a habit of reviewing your Journal on a regular basis. You might like to review it once a month and also update it whenever there's any change in your health. This means your Journal is always up-to-date so even if you're incapacitated, all the important details about your health are available to anyone who needs them.

Finally, I want to congratulate you on your decision to take charge of your own health and I wish you and your family good health for many years to come.

IN 90 SECONDS YOU CAN MAKE A HUGE DIFFERENCE

If you feel we've deserved it, please take a moment to leave a review on Amazon.

Your feedback means the world to us. It helps us to improve and it means better learning experiences for all our readers.

We'd be so grateful to you for your review!

Thank you!
Thank you!
Thank you!

REFERENCES

1. https://www.who.int/news-room/fact-sheets/detail/the-top-10-causes-of-death
2. PubMed.gov extract, 2017 https://pubmed.ncbi.nlm.nih.gov/28186008/
3. New Scientist, Aug 2017. https://www.newscientist.com/article/2143486-side-effects-kill-thousands-but-our-data-on-them-is-flawed/
4. https://www.nejm.org/doi/full/10.1056/NEJMp1302723
5. https://www.fsmb.org/siteassets/advocacy/news-releases/2018/harris-poll-executive-summary.pdf
6. https://www.nejm.org/doi/full/10.1056/nejmsa1012370
7. https://www.reuters.com/article/us-health-abortion-access-idUSKBN1XT2HA
8. https://www.ncbi.nlm.nih.gov/pmc/articles/PMC6455058/
9. https://pubmed.ncbi.nlm.nih.gov/15239078/
10. https://www.newscientist.com/article/2143486-side-effects-kill-thousands-but-our-data-on-them-is-flawed/#:~:text=As%20many%20as%2040%2C000%20people,full%20of%20noise%20and%20errors.
11. https://firstaidforlife.org.uk/first-aid/
12. https://www.bbc.co.uk/news/magazine-17013243
13. https://www.cdc.gov/heartdisease/facts.htm
14. https://www.heart.org/en/health-topics/heart-attack/treatment-of-a-heart-attack/aspirin-and-heart-disease
15. https://www.webmd.com/vitamins/ai/ingredientmono-662/turmeric#:~:text=Because%20curcumin%20and%20

References

other%20chemicals,that%20involve%20pain%20and%20inflammation.

16. https://www.everydayhealth.com/digestive-health/the-power-of-peppermint.aspx
17. https://www.wikihow.com/Ease-Peptic-Ulcers-Using-Bananas
18. https://www.mayoclinic.org/drugs-supplements/sodium-bicarbonate-oral-route-intravenous-route-subcutaneous-route/side-effects/drg-20065950
19. https://www.webmd.com/migraines-headaches/triggers-caffeine
20. https://pubmed.ncbi.nlm.nih.gov/26859020/
21. https://pubmed.ncbi.nlm.nih.gov/16802698/
22. https://pubmed.ncbi.nlm.nih.gov/21929329/
23. https://pubmed.ncbi.nlm.nih.gov/15239078/
24. https://emj.bmj.com/content/19/3/202
25. https://starship.org.nz/guidelines/paracetamol-poisoning/
26. https://www.kidney.org/news/kidneyCare/spring10/DietSoda
27. https://www.actiononsalt.org.uk/salthealth/salt-and-the-kidneys/
28. https://www.acs.org/content/acs/en/pressroom/presspacs/2016/acs-presspac-february-24-2016/too-much-salt-could-potentially-contribute-to-liver-damage.html
29. https://pubmed.ncbi.nlm.nih.gov/18184668/
30. https://www.mayoclinic.org/drugs-supplements-milk-thistle/art-20362885
31. https://www.nimh.nih.gov/health/statistics/schizophrenia
32. https://academic.oup.com/hmg/article/26/13/2462/3574683

33. https://www.unodc.org/documents/wdr/WDR_2010/2.0_Drug_statistics_and_Trends.pdf
34. https://www.cdc.gov/heartdisease/facts.htm
35. https://www.health.harvard.edu/heart-health/controlling-blood-pressure-with-fewer-side-effects
36. https://www.nhs.uk/conditions/heart-attack/causes/
37. https://www.cdc.gov/stroke/facts.htm
38. https://www.ncbi.nlm.nih.gov/books/NBK482514/
39. https://www.ncbi.nlm.nih.gov/pmc/articles/PMC3303565/
40. https://www.texasheart.org/heart-health/womens-heart-health/straight-talk-newsletter/weight-loss-products-and-heart-disease-there-is-no-silver-bullet/
41. https://www.cdc.gov/diabetes/library/spotlights/diabetes-facts-stats.html
42. https://www.ncbi.nlm.nih.gov/pmc/articles/PMC4549665/
43. https://www.ncbi.nlm.nih.gov/pmc/articles/PMC2586397/
44. https://journals.lww.com/md-journal/fulltext/2020/11060/ascorbic_acid_supplementation_in_type_2_diabetes.86.aspx
45. https://www.ncbi.nlm.nih.gov/pmc/articles/PMC3407731/
46. https://www.obesityaction.org/wp-content/uploads/Obesity-and-Stroke-Fact-Sheet.pdf
47. https://www.bhf.org.uk/informationsupport/risk-factors/obesity
48. https://www.ncbi.nlm.nih.gov/pmc/articles/PMC3066828/
49. https://www.ncbi.nlm.nih.gov/pmc/articles/PMC6734597/
50. https://www.cdc.gov/cancer/obesity/index.htm
51. https://www.health.harvard.edu/staying-healthy/should-you-try-the-keto-diet

References

52. https://www.heraldscotland.com/news/17456019.warning-diet-pills-blamed-26-deaths/
53. https://pubmed.ncbi.nlm.nih.gov/18392907/
54. https://www.cdc.gov/nchs/products/databriefs/db390.htm
55. https://www.nccih.nih.gov/health/acupuncture-in-depth
56. https://www.healthline.com/health/meditation-for-chronic-pain#new-paths
57. https://www.karger.com/Article/Abstract/335249
58. https://www.cochrane.org/CD009281/SYMPT_caffeine-analgesic-adjuvant-acute-pain-adults
59. https://www.fda.gov/drugs/drug-safety-and-availability/fda-recommends-avoiding-use-nsaids-pregnancy-20-weeks-or-later-because-they-can-result-low-amniotic#:~:text=The%20U.S.%20Food%20and%20Drug,the%20baby%20and%20possible%20complications.
60. https://www.nhs.uk/pregnancy/keeping-well/drinking-alcohol-while-pregnant/
61. https://www.cdc.gov/tobacco/campaign/tips/diseases/pregnancy.html
62. https://www.ncbi.nlm.nih.gov/pmc/articles/PMC4110809/
63. https://www.bannerhealth.com/healthcareblog/advise-me/is-it-safe-to-take-antibiotics-while-pregnant
64. https://doi.org/10.1001/jamapsychiatry.2019.3259
65. https://www.ncbi.nlm.nih.gov/pmc/articles/PMC4795985/
66. https://www.ncbi.nlm.nih.gov/pmc/articles/PMC4755634/
67. https://www.mayoclinic.org/diseases-conditions/morning-sickness/diagnosis-treatment/drc-20375260
68. https://www.ncbi.nlm.nih.gov/pmc/articles/PMC8801486/
69. https://kidshealth.org/en/parents/preg-folic-acid.html

70. https://www.healthline.com/health/food-nutrition/vitamin-b-complex#benefits
71. https://www.ncbi.nlm.nih.gov/pmc/articles/PMC3046737/
72. https://www.ncbi.nlm.nih.gov/pmc/articles/PMC5789217/
73. https://www.worldallergy.org/education-and-programs/education/allergic-disease-resource-center/professionals/vaccination-and-the-risk-of-atopy-and-asthma
74. https://www.gov.uk/vaccine-damage-payment
75. https://pubmed.ncbi.nlm.nih.gov/26004568/
76. https://www.mayoclinic.org/healthy-lifestyle/childrens-health/in-depth/cold-medicines/art-20047855
77. https://www.ncbi.nlm.nih.gov/books/NBK459224/
78. https://www.verywellhealth.com/what-is-causing-my-cough-1191888
79. https://www.medicalnewstoday.com/articles/318931
80. https://thorax.bmj.com/content/55/4/266
81. https://www.nidirect.gov.uk/articles/how-alcohol-affects-your-health#:~:text=to%20sudden%20death.-,Lungs,vomit%20gets%20into%20their%20lungs.
82. https://www.webmd.com/sleep-disorders/understanding-the-side-effects-of-sleeping-pills
83. https://pubmed.ncbi.nlm.nih.gov/19145994/
84. https://www.healthline.com/nutrition/does-vitamin-c-help-with-colds#TOC_TITLE_HDR_2
85. https://www.nccih.nih.gov/health/skin-conditions-at-a-glance
86. https://patient.info/news-and-features/how-do-skin-conditions-impact-mental-health
87. https://nationaleczema.org/eczema/

88. https://www.psoriasis.org/about-psoriasis/
89. https://www.nhs.uk/conditions/antibiotics/side-effects/
90. https://www.disabled-world.com/health/digestive/humanworms.php
91. https://www.thehealthsite.com/diseases-conditions/is-it-ok-to-take-medicines-with-soft-drinks-coffee-milk-or-juices-bs1017-527100/
92. https://www.tandfonline.com/doi/full/10.1080/16512235.2018.1548250
93. https://www.ncbi.nlm.nih.gov/pmc/articles/PMC2515351/
94. https://www.mayoclinic.org/diseases-conditions/peptic-ulcer/symptoms-causes/syc-20354223
95. https://pubmed.ncbi.nlm.nih.gov/20362756/
96. https://www.niddk.nih.gov/health-information/urologic-diseases/erectile-dysfunction/definition-facts#:~:text=ED%20is%20very%20common.,men%20in%20the%20United%20States.&text=Although%20erectile%20dysfunction%20(ED)%20is,health%20care%20professional%20about%20treatment.
97. https://www.mayoclinic.org/healthy-lifestyle/sexual-health/expert-answers/natural-aphrodisiacs/faq-20058252#:~:text=There's%20little%20evidence%20to%20support,sometimes%20claimed%20to%20affect%20libido.
98. https://www.news-medical.net/health/Obesity-and-Sexual-Health.aspx#:~:text=Obesity%20and%20reproductive%20functions,more%20likely%20to%20be%20infertile.
99. https://link.springer.com/article/10.1007/BF01541546?LI=true
100. https://www.ncbi.nlm.nih.gov/pmc/articles/PMC2978974/
101. https://www.nhs.uk/conditions/contraception/male-condoms/

102. https://www.nhs.uk/conditions/contraception/iud-coil/
103. https://www.plannedparenthood.org/learn/birth-control/birth-control-pill/how-effective-is-the-birth-control-pill
104. https://www.nhs.uk/conditions/contraception/contraceptive-implant/
105. https://www.cancer.gov/about-cancer/understanding/statistics#:~:text=Cancer%20is%20among%20the%20leading,related%20deaths%20to%2016.4%20million.
106. https://www.cancer.gov/about-cancer/understanding/statistics#:~:text=Prostate%2C%20lung%2C%20and%20colorectal%20cancers,diagnoses%20in%20women%20in%202020.
107. https://www.cancer.net/navigating-cancer-care/prevention-and-healthy-living/food-and-cancer-risk#:~:text=Processed%20meat%20includes%20bacon%2C%20ham,a%20higher%20risk%20of%20cancer.
108. https://www.mskcc.org/news/how-do-cigarettes-cause-cancer#:~:text=Scientists%20have%20known%20that%20smoking,could%20cause%20cancer%20in%20mice.
109. https://www.cancerresearchuk.org/about-cancer/causes-of-cancer/alcohol-and-cancer/does-alcohol-cause-cancer
110. https://cancercentersocal.com/uncategorized/link-sedentary-lifestyle-higher-cancer-risks/#:~:text=The%20link%20remains%20somewhat%20unclear,to%20cell%20growth%20in%20cancer.
111. https://www.healthline.com/nutrition/cancer-and-diet#:~:text=Higher%20consumption%20of%20foods%20rich,been%20linked%20to%20prostate%20cancer.
112. https://nutritionsimplified.co/blog-post/eating-better-but-feeling-worse
113. https://www.webmd.com/cancer/news/20170508/addressing-your-cancer-risk

References

114. https://www.cancerresearchuk.org/about-cancer/cancer-in-general/treatment/complementary-alternative-therapies/individual-therapies/vitamins-diet-supplements
115. https://www.cancer.gov/about-cancer/causes-prevention/genetics
116. https://www.mayoclinic.org/diseases-conditions/chemo-brain/symptoms-causes/syc-20351060#:~:text=Chemo%20brain%20is%20a%20common,cognitive%20impairment%20or%20cognitive%20dysfunction.
117. https://www.cancer.org/latest-news/facts-and-figures-2022.html#:~:text=The%20rate%20of%20localized%2Dstage,3%20years%20after%20their%20diagnosis.
118. https://medipense.com/top-10-reasons-seniors-do-not-take-their-medications/
119. https://www.ncbi.nlm.nih.gov/pmc/articles/PMC1947477/
120. https://www.everydayhealth.com/news/supplements-risks-every-women-should-know/
121. https://www.ncbi.nlm.nih.gov/pmc/articles/PMC6438434/#:~:text=In%20the%20current%20study%2C%20an,DHEA%2DS%20compared%20to%20placebo.
122. https://www.htc.co.uk/post/plant-power-for-hormonal-support#:~:text=One%20of%20the%20studies%20found,with%20relieving%20arthritis%2Drelated%20pain.
123. https://www.nccih.nih.gov/health/melatonin-what-you-need-to-know#:~:text=A%202019%20review%20looked%20at,fall%20asleep%20and%20total%20sleep.
124. https://pubmed.ncbi.nlm.nih.gov/2657105/#:~:text=oral%20yohimbine%20hydrochloride%20daily%2014,3%20weeks%20to%20manifest%20itself.

125. https://www.phoenix.ca/blog/spanish-fly-what-you-need-to-know-before-trying-it
126. https://www.ncbi.nlm.nih.gov/pmc/articles/PMC5949172/
127. https://www.ncbi.nlm.nih.gov/pmc/articles/PMC5628357/#:~:text=Ginseng%20shows%20superior%20regulation%20of,as%20swimming%20and%20immobilization%20tests.
128. https://www.ncbi.nlm.nih.gov/pmc/articles/PMC5481805/
129. https://www.nccih.nih.gov/health/st-johns-wort-and-depression-in-depth#:~:text=A%202008%20review%20of%2029,side%20effects%20than%20standard%20antidepressants.
130. https://www.ncbi.nlm.nih.gov/pmc/articles/PMC5548066/#:~:text=Fiber%20supplementation%20in%20the%20treatment%20of%20IBS,-Physicians%20(particularly%20those&text=A%20recent%20meta%2Danalysis%20that,compared%20to%20placebo%20(46).
131. https://www.pharmacytoday.org/article/S1042-0991(21)00837-9/fulltext#:~:text=A%202020%20review%20in%20Advances,reduction%20in%20liver%2Drelated%20deaths.